Rural Wisdom

by Larry J. Ernster

The Times When Life Has Really Spun Our Wheels

Understanding today's events from the
perspective of country wisdom.

Bloomington, IN   Milton Keynes, UK

authorHOUSE®

AuthorHouse™
1663 Liberty Drive, Suite 200
Bloomington, IN 47403
www.authorhouse.com
Phone: 1-800-839-8640

AuthorHouse™ UK Ltd.
500 Avebury Boulevard
Central Milton Keynes, MK9 2BE
www.authorhouse.co.uk
Phone: 08001974150

First published by AuthorHouse 11/1/2006

ISBN: 1-4259-5586-X (sc)
ISBN: 1-4259-5585-1 (dj)

Library of Congress Control Number: 2006907862

Printed in the United States of America
Bloomington, Indiana

This book is printed on acid-free paper.

Author's Note

Dear Reader,

In today's uncertain times I offer a quieter moment that takes you back and reminds you of when life was simpler and full of humor and love. This collection of essays and short stories centers on how rural wisdom is of value in today's city life. Having been raised in a large family on a small Minnesota dairy farm, this collection developed as I tried to understand today's events from the perspective of country wisdom. For example, in the story, "A Nose by Any Other Name," I found that the initial jarring my mind took when I came face-to-face with my first nose ring triggered memories of the nose jewelry we used on the farm, that differences are only initially jarring, and, differences are often the refreshing high points of our lives.

In "The Swarm" the distraction of honeybees finds the value of family during the death of a loved one. In "The Orange Prince" a working farm cat offers a second chance at forgiveness. While in "The Prairie Trip" I discover that life is just a dream, and we must choose which dream to dream.

These stories don't preach or pontificate--they appreciate. They are light-hearted and humorous and have brought smiles and tears to my family who has encouraged me to share them with others. These stories hope to bring you a deeper appreciation of family, while capturing an instant in time we each deserved to have lived.

I am the fortunate victim of a stable childhood, growing up in a large, secure and loving family of eight brothers and sisters. Given that perspective, my comments should be taken with several grains of salt. With that caution and with my family's encouragement I offer **"Rural Wisdom."**

Enjoy,

Larry Ernster

Childhood memories are pliable, wispy things subject to moods and interpretation. Certainty or accuracy are second only to truth which is as sure as the remembering.

Dedication

This book is dedicated to my parents and siblings without whom I wouldn't have had anything to write about and more importantly, I wouldn't have wanted to.

Linus and Pernilla—our guides and inspiration

Duane—our source of wisdom

Alice—our source of enthusiasm

Larry—the family historian

John—our outer child and inventive spirit

David—our energy for "doing"

Mark—our community spirit

Rita—our family's voice

Jane—our keeper of traditions

We're a package.

Table of Contents

Foreword

Another holiday is over and as I leave the farm of my youth and return to my home in the city, I am pumped full of turkey, dressing, pies and all the goodness of family--good family. When I was growing up, I resented the ordinariness of my family. It was stable, secure, and comfortable. Since there were ten of us it was never lonely or uneventful. It was us. Then when I became a teenager, family was an embarrassment. Mom and Dad were country folk. True, they were thoughtful, kind, dependable, respected, loving and giving; but they were as boring as Mom's blue-ribbon, homemade bread. It was there every day, and I was bored with it. Give me some store-bought white bread without all that graininess, and you'd think I had been given candy.

Finally, at the age of seventeen, it was time for me to leave the family and the farm. I liked being on my own--going places, doing things, being an adult. However, I was never able to recreate the feeling of family; that feeling of home, of belonging. Sure, strangers treated me better than family, although they never treated me with love. Sure, strangers never interfered, although I'm not sure they cared. Sure, strangers took me for face value and gave me a fresh start, although they never asked who I was or what was my story.

So I banged around for years. I didn't write home. I didn't call. I was searching for something that was missing. I completed the military, graduated from college, and started a family before I discovered that what I was looking for was what I had left behind--family.

What I noticed in those searching years was that my family, Mom and Dad and all those siblings, weren't common and ordinary. They were rare, unique and extraordinary. I was raised in one of those impossible idyllic times, surrounded by idyllic (and sometimes impossible) people. It was country living at its best, because it was country living in family and in love.

This is a collection of stories and essays of how things should be, and how, for an instant in this miracle of life, it was.

Fair Time
(Change)

Fair Time
(Change)

"Larry, it's time to get up," Mom whispered into my room.

No. It couldn't be. I just got in bed. It was still dark outside--I was sure, but I wasn't going to open my eyes and check. I could risk waking up. Besides, it was only my first call. Actually my second, the first call came hours ago when my older brother Duane tried to get me up for milking. He gave up, and I had heard him leave the house followed by the excited yelping and barking of our dogs, Frisky and Snowball, when he sent them to bring the cows home for milking. They were great (good) farm dogs. Not always providing a classic "Lassie" performance, but they were concerned enough about delivering the cows. I lay there in the dark knowing I would get another call, hopefully many hours from now.

There is an inclination, a big inclination, actually one of the primary forces in the universe--it falls right after gravity, magnetism and the Vanderwall forces that hold this universe together--to stay where you are. A renowned scientist stated it as "a body at rest will remain at rest until his father forces him out of bed." I experienced this many times in many

1

different situations, not just when trying to wake up. I don't like change.

"Larry, get up," my big sister called as she walked past my room on her way downstairs.

Boy, nothing is more annoying than big sisters. Always bossing you around and beating you up, and they fight dirty. Well, I'm sure not going to get up at her command. Besides, it's still dark--I think.

I'm extra tired this morning. Yesterday was the first day of the county fair and being members of the Caledonia Champion Racers 4-H Club, we delivered our projects, our prize cows, horses, and sheep to the fair to be judged. Of course, I was not as ready as I could have been. My brothers and I had spent the summer working at NOT getting ready. Sure we played with the thought of winning the champion's purple ribbon, but mostly we dragged our feet when it came time to fill out the dairy production records and document the genealogy of our fair animals. For Mom and Dad, encouraging the eight of us to get ourselves ready for the fair was like herding chickens. We had no clue as to where we were going. When the herding stopped, we would immediately return to scratching in the dirt. Getting ready for the county fair was a lot of work. It seemed that the fair was far more important for Mom and Dad, than it was for me. Actually, the truth was that Mom and Dad had this old-fashioned idea that we might actually learn something despite our passive resistance to their encouragement. In the end they would often carry our limp bodies (and projects) over the finish line.

"Larry, everybody's up. We're going to the fair," my little sister bubbled, interrupting my sleep and jolting my limp body.

I discovered early in life that I wasn't a "morning person." I've heard of morning people: idyllic, heroic, wide-eyed gazelles, up like a shot, listening to the morning songs of birds, but I've never really "seen" a morning person. My eyes have always been closed. Morning is too much of a change. By the time I adjust to morning, it's over.

Some people embrace change. They look for the good, the excitement, the opportunity--they're really annoying.

I can handle change. I've watched the sun set, silhouetting the barn against an orange-red sky. I've watched the woods turn crystal white as hoarfrost formed on trees as I sat in the woods waiting for ghost deer. I've walked to the top of the bluffs overlooking the Hiawatha Valley at dusk to watch twilight arrive and turn the city below into an apron of diamonds. I can handle change--change that doesn't affect me.

"Larry, put on your old clothes this morning. I'll bring up your show clothes when I come," Mom urged from the doorway.

This morning was the judging. For cattle judging, the showman costume was white pants, white shoes, and white shirt. Except for the big green 4-leaf clover on the front of the T-shirt, I looked like a first communicant. Before judging, each and every cow and calf would need to be scrubbed from toe to tail. One year, dressed in my white showman costume, I waded in mud and crawled on my knees while cleaning hoofs, brushing underbellies, combing tails, bleaching stains and glossing coats. This I did to the second and third and fourth, and, and, and, tenth cow or calf, only to find the first ones had lain down and were a mess again. And, oh yeah--I was a mess too. Mom now held onto the hand-washed, bleached and ironed whites until the last minute.

I pulled the covers farther over my head. I hated judging. I hated to be judged. It could point out the possibility that I needed to change or improve. We all need change and require change. Me? I could endure anything for a while. It is like sticking your head under water to look at the fish. You won't become a fish. You won't stay, but it's an exciting change.

"Larry, time to eat. Mom says to get up now or you won't get to eat until dinner," brother Dave reported.

Back again? Boy, it's hard to get some sleep with siblings parading past to go to the bathroom. In my next life I'm going to ask for a bedroom farther from the bathroom. Who cares about breakfast? I'd rather eat buttered popcorn and hot dogs at the fair, I thought from under the covers.

We often make bad choices when we choose the easy path. Avoidance of change will do that. Initially, doing nothing is easier. It is kind of like the frog sitting in a pot about to boil.

I only need a minute of sleep. If they'd just let me be.

In late August the county fair weather is deceiving. The days are hot and the nights are sticky, but the mornings are frigid. To parody Mark Twain, "The coldest winter I ever spent was an August morning at the fair." August is predictable, but you can't dress warm because it's going to be the hottest day of the year. This morning you'll look for frost as they drag you sleeping and limp to the fairgrounds to spray ice water on a grumpy cow who would rather be grazing and who has eyes on her butt so she can see to stomp on your toes.

"You missed breakfast. We're leaving," my big sister reported.

Good. Now I can get some sleep. The "townies" (the town kids) don't have to get up in the dark and the cold to shovel manure and make farm animals pretend they are having a good time. I want to be a townie and sleep until noon, or at least another five minutes.

I had learned to resist change while growing up in the small town of Caledonia, Minnesota. In Caledonia, from my childhood perspective, the town was divided between the Catholics and the non-Catholics. The non-Catholics included the Roman Catholics who attended St. John the Baptist Catholic Church. We called them the "Baptists." The "real" Catholics attended St. Peter's, since St. Peter was the rock upon which all of Catholicism was built, they were referred to as the "Rocks." The "Baptists" were primarily Irish, and the "Rocks" were primarily German/Luxembourg. Maybe it was an accident of geography (since we didn't have any real Baptists in town), but from my parochial view we considered our Catholic-Baptists only marginally Catholic.

We were magnanimous enough to allow their children to attend our Catholic Central Grade School, which was next to and supported by the real church of the Rocks. I viewed our invitation to them as a missionary attempt to convert their children to the "one true religion" centered on us Rocks.

"Larry, Dad's getting mad. We're all in the car waiting for you," my little brother pleaded.

Grownups always send kids to do things they're too lazy to do. "I'm getting up," I muttered from under the blankets. He stood there in the door. I didn't move or open my eyes. No need to. I knew it was dark. Finally I heard his footsteps go down the hall, down the stairs and the screen door slam.

"What's the rush?" I wondered justifiably annoyed. No need for me to hurry. My animals were clean and ready when I left them last night. I (well, actually my big brother Duane) had checked on them and had given them clean bedding, fed, watered and brushed them.

Procrastination is often an effective delaying tactic when presented with change. Procrastination's greatest supporter is "rationalization."

The problem of combining Caledonia's Catholic congregations (the Rocks and the Baptists) reached a crisis in the 1960's. There was a shortage of priests and our bishop, the revered Edward E. Fitzgerald, suggested the two parishes combine. After all, they were only two blocks apart. The bishop was suggesting change. The adults of both parishes felt threatened. Everyone could think of a reason for closing the "other" church and they bickered endlessly. No one took the bishop seriously.

After years of praying that the two parishes would come up with a plan for combining themselves, the bishop decided for them. At the front of each of these churches was a towering, stained-glass window that captured the essence of Peter the Rock and John the Baptist, each at the height of their spiritual life. The Bishop took these two glass icons and demoted both of them to smaller side windows and placed a new icon, St. Mary of Peace, in the big window at the head of the church. Today, years later, the Rock and the Baptist still stand face-to-face and glare at each other across the center aisle of St. Mary's. The losing church was quickly razed, and its quiet sanctuary of trees, grottos and church was turned into a parking lot and bank. The only known surviving relic is the communion railing that now decorates an establishment with the grand name of "Piggy's." Forty years later parishioners still consider themselves Baptists or Rocks. The reluctance to accept the forty-year-old change is generally well concealed until there is a problem--new change to consider. Then the two old parishes polarize and, of course, you expect the other side to think that narrowly.

"LARRY, GET UP!" yelled Dad from the car.

My eyes flew open. The sun was up. It was bright and I was wide-awake. I was late. I jumped into my clothes. I roared down the stairs and into the car before Dad's call echoed off the woods and faded down the valley. I was motivated.

A little motivation usually helps any change go down with less resistance. The challenge is finding the right motivation.

"Why didn't someone call me?" I complained as I climbed into the station wagon.

Indigent posturing will help you avoid admitting that a change was not as bad as you feared.

Cheeze, I hate change.

Of course, whining insures you won't learn from this.

Prairie Trip
(Choose a Dream)

The Prairie Trip
(Choose a Dream)

I've always admired Mom's appreciation of the little things in life: the warming sun, the discovery of a four-leaf clover, and the kindness of a friend. She tried to teach me that every moment in life is worthy of appreciation. Unfortunately, I still wait for the exceptional, the extraordinary, and the peak moments. They too are noteworthy. But I think Mom was trying to teach that it is the mundane, the ordinary, that enriches and makes us wealthy. If we children can learn to value these common moments and consider our richness, our lives would become the alchemist's gold transformed from lead. Each moment is an opportunity. Each instant is a treasure. Each turning is a gift returned.

Marriages, careers and lives are ended because of a lack of appreciation. And, as much as we resist our own responsibility, I've discovered that the appreciation we desire must come from within ourselves. Time and life come as opportunities for our appreciation. If we appreciate this moment, it is our initiative that generates the appreciation. If we feel appreciated, it is not because life has suddenly appreciated us, but because we are experiencing our appreciation of life. Similarly, if we appreciate our marriages, careers and the lives that populate them, we will feel the appreciation we give.

Well, sometimes I forget. So I sit here this morning neither appreciating, nor feeling appreciated, but contemplating how to reverse this negative mental spiral and wanting to be somewhere else.

Driving is useful when you want to be somewhere else. I'm heading west across the Minnesota prairie to visit my daughter, Miki. That's four hours of driving. It will be five, maybe six hours for me counting a sandwich and a nap or two. This time I'm taking the back roads. It is just an ordinary country road: black topped, two-laned, tree-lined (where there aren't cornfields), winding, ambling, comfortable, and with an occasional car or tractor.

I have everything a guy needs: a destination, a deadline and the time to get there. I'm a man with a mission. No time to dilly-dally. Although I want to get to my daughter's, each intersection on this picturesque, yellow-stripped, asphalt roller coaster, pulls at me. As I drive through intersections, there is a tug, like standing knee-deep in a rushing stream. It is a tug inviting me to follow left or right. I stick to my straight-ahead destination, but I wonder what adventures, what scenery, what stories would be down that dusty gravel road, on the far side of the three-hump road, or around the bend where the road is bent around the farmhouse?

Here in the country the roads are still meant to serve its inhabitants. The roads go around the farmhouses and wander left or right to find towns truly in the middle of nowhere. The Interstate is meant to serve strangers; to help them avoid the country. It cuts an efficient swath across the country and rolls over farms instead of around them. It goes past towns instead of through them. Country folk don't have any use for the Interstate. By the time they drive to the Interstate, down the frontage road and loop-de-loop the cloverleaf, and repeat the process getting off, they could have driven there and back twice. The Interstate serves strangers. The back roads serve the inhabitants.

It's early October and as I drive this ribbon of smooth asphalt that now stretches straight ahead until it disappears into a mirage of water, I watch the corn being harvested and think of how harvesting has changed. I remember my Dad lamenting the disappearance of the horse and the corn shocks, and how he almost won the corn-husking contest at the county fair. In corn-husking contests each contestant was given a bushel of corn with the husks still on the corn. Contestants were timed de-husking their bushel of corn.

Forever, during my youth, there were corn-husker gloves hanging from the corncrib. Every couple of years, I'd ask again what they were, and Dad would put them on and demonstrate how they worked. His demonstration was always compromised. There was no corn to husk (or de-husk). Mechanical corn pickers with rollers snapped ear-corn clean off the stock and husk, and heaped big wagons with clean golden ears. Gone were small wagons drawn by a team of workhorses. Gone were the wagons filled with corn still in the husk. Gone were the daylong conversations between horse and man as they worked their way across the field, stripping the corn from the stock by hand and lofting it toward the wagon.

Corn picking by hand was a mindless, grueling activity. Humans reduced to work horses, working as one of the team as the three of them worked the field. The horses started and stopped on voice commands, and returned to the home buildings only to unload or for darkness that came earlier each frosty day.

Each generation has its own music that attaches itself to the psyche during youth. Whether it is swing or ragtime, country or rock and roll, punk or rap, the music strikes a cord with its personal meaning and the memories it recalls for each generation.

Just as each generation has its own music that attaches to the psyche during youth, so do the experiences and the trappings of youth attach to the psyche. For my Dad one such detail was the small horse-drawn wagon of husked corn. For me it was the larger wagons heaped full of large yellow ears. Today, as I cross the prairie, I notice those wagons of large yellow ears of corn are gone also. They have been replaced by combines that pick and shell the corn, spitting both the cob and the husks back into the field in a trailing cloud of chaff as the combine collects the harvest six, eight or ten rows at a time.

Economics drives this efficiency. Efficiency has been labeled progress.

Progress--I'm still on course to my daughter's, and the mile-marking side roads still tug at me, still promise adventures, but I continue.

Now, if corn-picking progress had stopped with my Dad's experience, I never would have ridden in the big wagon being pulled behind the corn picker, with the corn picker throwing clean ears into the wagon faster than I could count. I never would have fallen asleep, safe under the wagon, only waking when the wagon passed over the top of me. I woke under a cold October starry night needing to chase the wagon like a stagecoach bandit and climb into the back of the moving wagon.

I scolded my big brother for driving off with me under the wagon. He said something about that being a pretty stupid place to sleep, and why wasn't I helping instead of sleeping?

We quit after that load, at least I did. The good-news-bad-news of the tractor was its lights which allowed you to work well past sunset, or even all night.

Today the mechanical corn pickers that proud tractors wore like suits of armor are gone. Today monster combines pour rivers of shelled corn into waiting trucks without stopping to rest. One great combine nurses a whole litter of trucks, each truck taking a turn at the augured feeding tube. The trucks offering their yawning mouths like blind baby birds demanding to be fed or suckled until their bellies are bloated. Satisfied, the trucks trundle slowly across the field leaving heavy tracks in the spongy earth.

It seems too easy.

I can declare this generation of farmers too mechanized and too detached from the real love of the soil; but, ironically, that is how my father felt about my generation's farming techniques. If you ask the lads driving the machinery today, they would be surprised at my claims that they have distanced themselves from real farming. Like their fathers and grandfathers, today's farmers work the same eighteen-hour days in the spring and fall. They make hay when the sun shines and thank God when it rains. They just do more of it which is an accident of technology.

Today there is plenty to appreciate. Today the sun shines for some youth integrating today's music, today's technology, today's possibilities into his or her psyche. I have shared this day and can appreciate their experience and receive the appreciation we each deserve but must first give. Appreciation (if you will allow me to steal another's metaphor) is like sitting in front of a stove demanding heat. saying, "You give me heat, then I'll give you wood." You have to be the first to give. The first to appreciate.

And now I feel warmed. Warmed by the sun now in the West turning the autumn leaves to gold and crimson, pastels and vibrant dayglow colors, colors of warm browns and fresh greens. This time of day the common becomes magic. The setting sun filters through a milkweed pod's gauzy beard that waits for the next wind to carry its seeds and its possibilities to a new tomorrow. Even the dust trailing the combine takes on a magical look as the lowering sun catches it and follows the dust gently back to earth.

Surprisingly, my funk is gone. My spiral has been reversed and I feel blessed, blessed that I was given this day, this life, this opportunity to appreciate. Interesting--nothing has changed. I have not spoken to a soul all day (save the speakerphone at McDonald's drive through), and yet I feel rejuvenated, refreshed, alive and appreciated. I never did chase one of the dreams down the side roads that tugged at me as I passed. I know any one of them would have been fine, but so too is the straight road I took. True, I may have missed an opportunity for a different dream, but if I had chosen differently I'd be missing the dream I'm dreaming.

Interesting--life is ever amazing.

Ring of Fingers
(Choices We Make)

It was a normal day at work: slaying dragons, rescuing fair maidens, and counting the king's money. I arrived home and stabled my noble steed named Cavalier. Princess Mary Kris, my wife, met me at our castle door with a worried look. The look was troubling enough to be a family death, a terrible injury, or a personal trauma. It was personal trauma. A dragon was discovered living in our happy home. Our happy home was now his happy home. Actually "mouse sign" was discovered--little chocolate donut sprinkles had appeared in the bottom of our kitchen cupboards.

Mouse. What was I going to do about it? Although Mary Kris didn't say so directly, I felt accused of inviting the little beggar in.

One little mouse can't be that hard to trap. We had lots of traps on the farm. Most of them hung rusting behind the shop door. Mostly there were gopher traps, but we had larger ones for fox and badger. We could trap just about anything for which we could set a trap. As kids, my brother John and I would wrestle with these bigger traps trying to set them. It took the both of us. One stood on the springs, the other (the unlucky one) stuck a hand in the trap and set the trigger. Since I was bigger and heavier, John set the trigger. John almost got the nickname "Stubs" as we attempted to set these traps. I was almost heavy enough to open the jaws. By jumping on the springs I could collapse them enough for the jaws to open. John wasn't fast enough to stick his hand in the jaws and catch the trigger before the spring would catapult me off, slamming the jaws shut. If we could have set the trap, we could have caught all sorts of wild beasts. Forty years later, that trap is probably still hanging there waiting for someone heavy enough to set it. I could probably set it now.

For an experienced trapper like myself, one little mouse would be easy. I went to the hardware store and bought the traditional head-banger traps. These I distributed around the house. Each offered a different snack of sunflower seeds, various cheeses, butter, peanut butter, rice, or jams. Nothing happened. Either the mouse did not recognize my treats as food, or he did not want a headache. The mouse never touched my trap treats.

Being an advocate of new technology I resorted to the flypaper technique. If I couldn't get the mouse to eat, maybe he/she would scurry across a sticky trap.

Nothing.

The only thing I caught was the family dog. I heard a great deal of flopping and moaning and came to find Rusty, our old dog, stuck like brer Rabbit to a tar-baby. When I walked in he gave me the "Help, I've fallen and can't get up" look.

For two weeks Mary Kris wouldn't go into her home office and work. She would stand in the hallway outside her office, make announcing noises, spot some needed tool or paper from the doorway, then make a beeline in and out of the office before the little furry guy had a chance to scurry up her leg.

* * *

Late one night we're lying in bed. I'm sleeping. Then I'm getting poked. "Whaaat?" I said.

"Shhh. Do you hear that?" Mary Kris said.

I listened to the quiet interrupted only by the rumbling purring of the cat. "Whaaat?" I asked in my most caring voice.

"The mouse--he's here in our bedroom." Her arm was now around me. It had the flexibility of a crowbar. We lay there listening to the silence.

"Whaaat?" The crowbar was pounding on my chest.

"There. By the dresser." We listened.

I tried to get up. The crowbar tightened. "I'm not leaving." The crowbar relaxed. I picked the family cat up off of the bed and set her down next to the dresser. The cat back-peddled and jumped back onto the bed. A second time I set the cat in front of the dresser. The cat skedaddled.

"Where's Baby?"

That's the problem with names. A cat should be named Claw or Sting or Killer or Mouser. A cat named "Baby" bears no malice toward other living creatures. "She's cowering by the head of the bed. I don't think she is going to be any help."

The hearing ability of women must increase in the dark. Mary Kris woke me again in the smallest hours of the night. She whacked me with the crowbar. "Listen!"

"Whaaa?"

"Shhh. It's by the wall. No it's behind the wall."

I would have thought that if the little critter was on the other side of the wall, Mary Kris would feel less threatened--safer. Instead, her's was a horror film response. It was that suspenseful moment just before the ax murderer breaks through the wall and attacks. The ax murderer was scratching, quiet as a mouse, searching for a weak spot to come exploding through. Mary Kris has got to stop reading those murder mysteries.

"Go see," she pleads.

I unbend the crowbar from across my chest and go in the dark to the spot on wall where she points. Sure enough, I hear the ax murderer scratching away behind the wall. "Hmmm. You're right. It's behind the wall." I go back to bed.

"No. Take off the molding."

"I thought you didn't want him in here?"

"I don't. I want him out of there."

Maybe it was late. Maybe I was tired. The logic escaped me, and I went back to the wall and squatted down, staring at the quiet where the scratching was. "I'm not really dressed for tearing the wall apart." I waited at the wall like a cat at a mousehole. (Not our cat, but like you'd want a cat to wait.) I wondered if I slept in this position, with my knees in my armpits, if I'd still be able to walk in the morning. Quiet followed quiet. If I could find the mouse hole, I could use Mom's ring-of-fingers technique for catching stripped gophers. This was done by making a two-handed circle with her thumbs and forefingers and placing them over the gopher hole. Then she waited while her big brothers (Willy, Sy and Lee) dashed back and forth to the hand pump, delivering buckets of water that they poured through her ring of fingers, down into the gopher hole. When the gopher came gasping out of the hole to complain, he would pop up into Mom's waiting ring of fingers where she would wring his half-drowned neck. She did this barehanded. I would advance the technique by using gloves. Mary Kris would dash back and forth to the sink carrying five-quart ice cream buckets of water. These she would pour down the mouse hole through my leathered fingers while I waited for the wall to fill up and flush the little guy up into my waiting, leathered, ring of fingers. Maybe tomorrow.

Finally I unfolded the best I could and stumbled back into bed waking the cat. Mary Kris put her arm around me. "I think you're safe," I said moving the crowbar from my windpipe to across my chest.

The alarm clock went off, and Mary Kris was relating a dream she woke with. In the dream the mouse sprang from the top of the chair, to the nightstand, to right on top of her. No, she couldn't remember what the mouse did once he got there. No. She didn't know why the mouse would want to do that.

This mouse was really starting to annoy me.

* * *

I saw the mouse today. I was sitting right here at the computer, and a small gray blur caught the corner of my eye. The mouse ran across my home office floor, within an inch of our sleeping dog, and disappeared behind the books stacked on the floor. I dashed out of the room to the hall closet and got my leather work gloves. I was going in after him. What I learned from years on the farm is that these critters are armed to the teeth--or with teeth. If I was going to have hand-to-hand combat with a mouse, I needed body armor. Unless the mouse violated the rules of fair play and ran up my pants leg, the gloves should suffice.

Before I could begin disassembling the pile of books I had to clear a space on the floor. This meant waking the watchdog. Rusty was an old dog, prone to sleeping twenty some hours a day. Waking him for lunch wasn't always easy. Waking him at midnight for no good reason wasn't on his agenda. Sure he was a watchdog, but he had watched for seventeen years and nothing had happened. This midnight, he was not amused when I asked him to move. He walked three steps, going under Mary Kris' desk, and dropped back to the carpet with an annoyed sigh.

Being deaf with failing vision, Rusty was not interested in my complaint that he didn't catch the mouse.

I moved all the books. I was ready; ready to pounce on the mouse. After the last book had been moved and all empty cracks and corners explored without finding a mouse, I noticed how tense I was. Did I mention that this mouse was starting to annoy me? I replaced the books, and wondered how the little critter disappeared.

A couple nights later I went through the same drill. The dog is on the floor. I'm on the computer. The mouse dashes past. He must have a route--a mouse route. Discovering the trails of wild animals was always the first step in trapping them. Once you know the route you can set a trap or snare on the trail. Rabbits were often my quarry. They frequented the arching barbs of blackberry patches, and the burdock-filled corners of our fields. In the winter it was easy to spot the trails that their soft snowshoe feet had stomped into the snow. A simple noose draped across the trail and tied to the trunk of a burdock was an almost guaranteed way to snare a rabbit. The rabbit would hop down the trail right though the noose that would tighten around the neck and Wallah--pet rabbit. This technique never did work for me. I figured the rabbit's ears kept getting in the way. I wondered how big a noose I needed for a mouse?

I went looking for string.

* * *

Today Mary Kris had her first glimpse of the mouse. For a couple weeks the mouse has been ignoring my treats of seeds, jam and cheese that I set out in the finger-snapper traps. He's been walking around my sticky traps to get to the good stuff. Like most homes we keep our trash in a paper bag under the kitchen sink. Every day the mouse would chew a hole in the paper bag and gorge himself on leftovers. The shredded paper and chocolate sprinkles left behind, distressed Mary Kris. From the mess she figured it was a guy mouse.

Mary Kris, not wanting to interrupt the little guy in mid-feast, always knocked on the cabinet door and shouted announcements like, "I'm opening the door," before tossing away trash. Or she'd stage the trash on the top of the counter waiting for me to open the door and defeat any dragons lurking within.

Today she forgot and opened the door without knocking. The mouse was busily trying to pull a too-big piece of pepperoni pizza out the mouse hole he had chewed in the bag. Caught in mid-burglary, the excitement started. Mary Kris slammed the cabinet door so hard it bounced open again. The slamming door sounded like a gunshot to the mouse and me. The startled mouse let go of the pizza and tumbled onto the kitchen floor. Mary Kris, seeing the door pop open, slammed it shut accidentally locking the mouse out of his cabinet in front of the dog and cat. The cat disappeared like one of those cartoon animals leaving behind only a cloud of shedding cat hair settling onto the kitchen floor. The dog's ears perked up for just an instant before he returned to his nap.

I spied the mouse on the floor and dropped to all fours to match him in mortal hand-to-hand combat. The mouse was dashing left, then right, like an indecisive squirrel in front of an oncoming truck. I was the truck, and I was going to take him out. I lunged after the mouse. It was more of a feint, when I remembered I wasn't wearing any body armor. I backed off. The mouse seeing an opening dashed under the kitchen table and headed for the basement steps.

Angered that the mouse was about to escape I went down the stairs three steps at a time. I was able to get ahead of the mouse. I think stairs were a new obstacle course for the mouse. On each step he would run left, then right, the width of the stair before going down one more step and then repeat the process. I was ahead of the mouse. The overhang on each step prevented him from going back up.

I was still without body armor (also known as heavy leather gloves), and the mouse and I squared off. He was three steps above me. We were eye to eye. He gave me a quick fake to the left and dove right past me. I slammed a forearm down to crush him while Mary Kris, the fair maiden whose colors I wore in this hand-to-paw joust, cheered from the upstairs landing.

Surely, the battle was ended. My foe was surely crushed beneath my massive forearm. Gingerly I peeked under the sleeve. Nothing. Then I saw the mouse. In an astonishingly brilliant move he had swerved from under my crushing forearm and had wedged himself against the wall, between the molding and the carpeting. Well, same result. He is cornered, captured and must capitulate.

As I knelt there wondering how to transfer the mouse to the outside, my fair maiden cautioned, "Things that touch terror shall never touch mine," and she left to get some paper towels. At that very instant the mouse sprang from his safety under the molding and finished the steps three at a time. He had apparently watched me come down after him. I shouted, "Hey! Come back here." and felt a little stupid for the comment. The mouse disappeared quicker than cheese on a mousetrap (not my mousetraps, but like you'd expect cheese to disappear.)

The dragon escaped. The basement now became a place of horrors that my fair maiden was loath to enter.

I returned to the hardware store and headed to the mousetrap department. I ignored the traps. They had all failed. This was a city mouse raised around traps. Mice are trainable. This mouse is smart. It took him just one example to learn about steps. I had decided to resort to chemical warfare. I know the Geneva Convention had banned chemical warfare. Nerve gas, biological weapons and poisons were not considered fair, but there I was resorting to poisons. Hardware stores are a virtual weapons depot of chemical weapons. You need but select a victim (weed, insect, or critter) and decide on the flavor and form of the weapon. I chose an inviting box in the shape of a cheese wedge and left.

We really have only three choices in life: Good, Bad or OK. We think we can control life and make things the way we want. And it's true that we can affect circumstances, and we can contrive outcomes; but in the end, after all our plotting and manipulating we end up where we are--not where we planned, and we must declare where we are to be: Good, Bad or OK.

Well, our house is quiet again. There are no dragons lurking in our cupboards, and that's Good. I do feel that I violated the Geneva Convention by resorting to poisons, and that's Bad. But, a man must protect his home, so it's OK. And now my home is safe for fair maidens, and that's Great!

A Lot of Bull
(We All Want the Same Things)

A Lot of Bull
(We All Want the Same Things)

Growing up on the farm, we lived in a world without danger. True, there was the annual story of the farmer who fed himself into a hay bailer, the persistent autumn loss of arms snapped off in the rollers of corn pickers, and the summertime loss of legs torn off in unguarded power-take-off shafts. True enough, there were heights to fall from, and pitchforks to fall on, but these were benign dangers that were just part of the time and rural culture. Few farmers made it through their life's work without cutting off at least one body part. But there was no 911 and color-coded security alerts. There were no dangers that pursued you aggressively--that intended you harm.

However, in the midst of my boyhood perfect peace and serenity there was the bull.

Farms have lots of cows. Each farm generally settles on just one type of cow: dairy cows, beef cows, white cows, or brown cows. Our farm went through several iterations of cows. When I was young, we were a Guernsey herd. Guernsey cows are medium-sized, brown and white cows with wonderful dispositions. We considered them the best breed of cows in the world. We touted their merits with religious fervor, as fiercely as we defended the red Farmall tractors against the green putt-putt John Deere tractors. My Uncle Julius, however, raised the huge black and white Holsteins and drove an unremarkable gray Ford tractor.

The good-natured family feuding over which breed of cow was best was as fierce as the popcorn wars between my Dad, Linus and his brother, Julius. My Dad favored the smaller white popcorn, while Julius, the older and bigger brother, favored the yellow, larger puffed kernel of corn. Each fall the popcorn would be harvested and secretly dried and cured in preparation for a corn-popping challenge. The winner was declared by having the fewest number of old maids (unpopped kernels) in the bottom of each pan. Having a complete popping (no old maids) was the seldom-achieved goal. The drying of the harvested ears of popcorn was the secret. Popcorn kernels explode when the moisture inside the kernel is heated to steam. If the kernels are too dry, they don't pop. If they are too damp, the husk of the kernel will be too soft and leak the steam before it reaches popping pressure.

Then one day, one of Julius' black and white Holsteins got mixed up in our Guernsey herd. Within a couple years, our entire herd turned black and white. It was unsettling for us as kids. We used to kick-butt on the school playground proving that Guernsey cows were better than Holsteins and now we were Holsteins. Then about the time we had embraced the glories of the big black and whites, my Dad, in search of the perfect cow, discovered the Ayrshire. Personally, I always thought that the Ayrshire was just a red and white Holstein with horns. The breed was nearly as big as the Holsteins and came with spectacular horns that were suitable for trophy mounting in your den. We didn't have a den on the farm, and except for a set on the front of our pickup, we left the horns on the Ayrshire as our farm underwent another changeover and the black and whites were carted off to the sales barn and replaced with red and whites.

Up to this time our farm had no bull. We (the collective family we) were advocates of artificial insemination. We adamantly advocated artificial insemination just as staunchly as we supported red tractors and red and white cows. An important requirement of artificial insemination is that you become aware of the cow's mood. You need to know from her actions when she is impregnable. Semen was expensive and you didn't want the artificial inseminator to make a wasted trip. So you'd pay close attention to Bossy's relationships with other cows and the timing of her lactation cycle. When Bossy pined for the Big Guy, you only have a couple days to get the Big-Guy-in-a-Bottle to show up with his panel truck, rubber boots and long rubber glove. The benefit of needing to be in sync with a whole herd of moody females is that you realize that there are times that are right, and times when she'll kick your head off. Then the guy with the long rubber glove will chastise you for having him make the long drive up the driveway only to be abused.

When I was young and into my teens, our farm had only female animals. We had chickens, but no roosters; horses, but no stallions; and, cows but no bulls. I remember that my sex education went something like this: "Dad, where do babies come from?"

"Go out in the barn and look."

Unfortunately the barn held only half of the story. There were dozens of females, but no males, and yet babies regularly appeared. Every spring new foals could be found standing on brand-new wobbly legs getting their first milk, and baby chicks by the hundreds showed up in cardboard boxes. Since a significant part of the story of procreation was missing from the barn, my understanding of the whole process was a mite twisted. It was always celebration or sorrow at a birth. If it was female, that was great. But if it was a bull calf or a stud colt, within a month he was carted off to the sales barn for a very short trip to the cannery or the fox farm. It seemed we went out of our way to guarantee all male animals a bad time.

With chickens, male expulsion was a little different. It is nearly impossible to visually determine the sex of a baby chicken. There was rumor of the occupation of "chick sexer." This was someone who could divine the sex of a chick and separate the future hens from the future roosters. Then, when you purchased your flat of chicks, you would be willing to pay more for a box of chicks being assured that you would get mostly hens. Dad was determined to cull the flock of all roosters. As far as I could tell, a rooster-less flock was preferred for the same reason we drove red tractors. So we watched the chicks grow and as soon as the chicks started losing their cute yellow fluff and started growing pin feathers we could spot the rooster's bright red comb. Like most birds, the males are the more colorful and with all white chickens, that meant the bigger comb on the top of their heads. Once the combs appeared, Dad calculated that the chick sexer was right about 50% of the time.

Having a bunch of young roosters in the flock was not a bad thing since it was only temporary. Roosters were allowed to hang out on the farm a bit longer than other males, but just before the pullets began their lives of egg-laying, all the roosters passed over the chopping block and became Sunday dinner.

On the farm we were downright hostile to the male animal. The rituals for purifying the farm were different for each species and ranged from exile, to de-masculinzation, to murder. That was why the appearance of Clyde the bull was such an event.

To work with the cows my older brother Duane had two matching white German Shepherd dogs named Poopsie and Mitzi. They formed a trio that went everywhere together. They followed Duane from one end of the farm to the other until they dropped Duane at the farmhouse doorstep in the evening. The next morning they would greet Duane where they left him and with a few simple words and some hand signals from Duane, the three of them would herd the cows from pasture to barn for their twice-a-day milking. Clyde the bull was among the herd. Even though Clyde wasn't necessary for the milkings he followed along, lording over his harem, always keeping them within sight. Even when they entered the barn, and the Shepherds kept him out, Clyde would watch his ladies through the half-door or the window unless there was someone more interesting in the barnyard.

Bulls are notoriously protective of their herds. Nature gave bulls this disposition to protect the herd from predators and from less-dominant suitors. Bulls were given two primary defenses: their horns and their massive heads. Most people fear the horns with good reason. But getting gored by a bull is preferable to being crushed by his massive head. If a bull catches you by its horns, you'll probably be thrown ten feet and be able to get up and run away. But the bull's most deadly weapon is its crushing head. He uses its mass to pin whoever defiled his turf and crush every bone until all life is forced out. Our great uncle was killed that way.

The other reason bulls are so dangerous is that they are unpredictable. As a farmer, you work with these animals every day and you think you know their temperament and they know and trust you, and you can be lulled into a false trust.

My older brother Duane had a good relationship with Clyde. Clyde could be led and fed and scratched, and he seemed downright docile. Duane felt that he had no worries because his two German Shepherds (Poopsie and Mitzi) were always by his side, and they kept Clyde in line.

But you never know what sets a bull off. Like the time my sister Rita met the bull on the lane to the woods. She ran. The bull chased. Then the two of them played ring-around-the-hickory-nut-tree until Duane arrived on a tractor to pick her up. While the rescue wasn't as romantic as a prince on a white horse swooping her out of harm's way, when the tractor arrived, Rita didn't wait for a better offer.

Then you can always go out of your way to aggravate a bull. Baby sister Jane has always used the direct approach to life. When a bull refused to go through a gate, Jane, from the safety of horseback, kicked him in the butt. A tolerant bull will endure one insult, but when Jane delivered the second kick-in-the-butt, the head dropped, the nostrils flared, and the bull charged. Luckily, Jane was astride Pretzels the cow pony. Pretzels, seeing the charging bull, did an airborne ninety-degree pivot and planted a nicely trimmed hoof neatly between the bull's eyes, forever giving new meaning to the term "bull's eye." The bull stopped in his tracks, shook his head, and decided he really did want to go through the gate after all.

You never know what sets a bull off. You can be sure it was something the bull perceived as a threat to his harem. But maybe he just harbors resentment from the demeaning treatment from the Shepherds, or the twice-a-day separation from his harem during milking, or perhaps it was a springing heifer coming into heat that fired Clyde's testosterone when Duane entered the barnyard without his Shepherds.

As Duane crossed the barnyard carrying a battery charger for the ailing tractor hooked to the manure spreader, Clyde came after Duane. Duane threw the battery charger at Clyde. Clyde easily avoided the battery charger and kept coming. Clyde had been slightly disarmed. His two-inch thick, four-foot long horns had been aborted at birth by the application of acid on the "horn seeds" on either side of his head. This was a standard farm practice and left a slightly deformed head.

Rather than a natural triangular head, all bovine that have had their horns removed by acid have a "kite-shaped" head--kind of pointy at the top. This was Clyde's profile.

Then Duane did the one thing you don't want to do when you are being chased by a pointy-headed bull--stumble. At that moment it didn't matter to Clyde that it was Duane who cared and tended for him and his harem, or that is was Duane who made Clyde's idyllic life of grazing and mating possible, Duane was down.

If you've seen a bull attack, the battering ram and horns are used to "down" their victim. The kill is the crush. Once a bull pins his victim beneath his massive head, he transfers his full weight into the crush until no struggle remains.

Duane landed in a lump, but with his senses intact. He rolled over and saw the crush coming. He tried to get up and the battering ram hit him sending him rolling toward the fence. The crush moved in, and Duane rolled out from under it. The crush kept approaching, and Duane kept rolling over to the hog-wire barbed-wire fence surrounding the barnyard, and now he was trapped against the fence face up. He couldn't roll over to get his feet under him without rolling back into the barnyard. He couldn't get up, and he couldn't roll under the fence. The crush was within inches and coming fast. The barbed-wire hog-wire fence was a barrier between Duane and safety. From where he lay, Duane could see safety; even touch safety through the rusted-wire lattice work.

The mind is an amazing tool, and inspiration is astounding. In the fraction of seconds available to save him, Duane noticed an electric-fence wire a couple feet above his head. It was bound to a white ceramic cylinder, an electric insulator.

Fencing around farms is often evolutionary and layered. Fencing changes to accommodate changes in livestock. When old fencing falls down, it is often not removed, but repaired and patched until you have Duane lying against a hog-wire, barbed-wire, electric-wire fence that generally, but not always, kept the cows on the intended side.

As the crush came in for the kill, Duane pulled the metal rod electric fence-post out of the ground, and using it like Prince Valiant's sword, shoved the attached electric wire into Clyde's descending face.

You can never defeat a bull. Their temperament will not acknowledge defeat. They do, however, have short attention spans. The electric fence zapped Clyde on the nose, and he forgot why he was upset with Duane and ambled off to another part of the barnyard.

Duane, bruised and battered, was still on his back and pinned against the fence. He dropped the electric wire, rolled back into the barnyard to get his feet under him and went back to chores.

I expect Poopsie and Mitzi were apologetic about their lapse in duty. Clyde was given a one-way ticket to the big house for his actions, and future bulls were asked to drag a three-foot chain from their noses. The hope was that if a bull put his head down to charge, he would step on the chain and stop the charge. Duane never mentioned the event. He considered it part of what he does. The story was exposed when Mom noticed Duane was black-and-blue from his neck to his knees.

Me? Where I grew up, I never considered security important. Where and when I grew up there were no malicious dangers, except bulls, and we knew where they were--or where they were supposed to be. We didn't lock our doors or take the keys out of our cars. That's the way life should be. We should be so secure that security is not an issue or a consideration. Safety, however, should be an on-going concern if we expect to keep from losing important body parts. Wars should be restricted to "popcorn wars" where the only explosions are the vigorous popping of the corn. Arguments should be enthusiastic and confined to the color of your tractor, not the color of your skin. And lastly, we should remember that the search for the perfect breed of cow (or the perfect religion) is still going on, and that whatever cow you're milking is providing sustenance for you and your family. Another family may choose a different cow, but that's OK because we all want the same things: to be healthy and happy, to be loved and appreciated, and to have the opportunity to contribute to life.

Cow Snoozing
(Things are the Way They're Supposed to Be)

Cow Snoozing
(Things are the Way They're Supposed to Be)

It was dark when I got home from work. Mary Kris, my wife, was already asleep so Rusty, our dog, and I plopped on the couch to share my dinner and watch TV. I watched TV. Rusty watched my dinner. He was complaining that I wasn't sharing fairly, so I sent him outside to check for midnight squirrels.

It was snowing glitter. It was one of those beautiful natural events like the sunsets artists capture on canvas that are so beautiful they look fake; so beautiful that even when you're standing in front of the real thing, it looks fake. I put Rusty out into the shower of glitter. The deck looked like one of those globes you shake, and glitter snows on a Christmas manger.

Rusty set off across the deck, and I stuck my hand out to catch the glitter. Fifty years ago I would have stepped out into the glitter, put my head back and caught them with my tongue. Tonight I'm content to feel flakes cold and biting on my wrist and melting like a fine spray on my hand.

It is January. January is the time of year we Minnesotans love most to brag about. True, we do it by complaining because we were taught that bragging was not allowed. Hence we complain about the things we're most proud. In January it's snow and cold. If we get a call from a relative down South who didn't get any snow, we don't brag about how much snow we got and rub his face in it (so to speak). No, we try to make the poor smuck feel OK about the crummy, tepid, unchanging weather they're probably having down South. So we complain. It's the only release we allow ourselves. After all, if we got too excited we could work up a sweat and freeze to death as soon as we calmed down.

It's winter, and it's supposed to be cold. Your body can tolerate being hot in the summer, but hot in the winter causes your body to revolt. Recently I've been waking in the middle of the night with my knees aching because I am hot--turkey roasting, bone-baking hot. I fear I'll burst into flames.

I throw off some of the heavy quilts. A merciful bit of cold air leaks in. I lie on my side and flail at the mountain of covers. I fold them back so that I'm only half covered. What I accomplished is that I now have twice the thickness of blankets on top of me with only the smallest crack of coolness.

My feet have reached their melting point. For some sadistic reason the family cat has developed great affection for my feet. It seems she can't sleep without them and must sleep on top of them. I wake in the middle of the night fearing my feet are being vibrated off my ankles, and at the last minute rescue them from under the cat and move them to another part of the bed. The cat complains and stalks my feet waiting for them to settle before curling up on, between, or around my feet. Being the only cat in the house I suspect she considers my feet a coil of cats, bundled up together on a cold winter's night. With all the blankets on my feet I can't get off a good, well-intended encouragement.

The best I can muster is to let the blankets form a pouch, like that in a slingshot, cradling the cat. Then using my legs like an apult (cat-apult), I free my feet from their furry booties. In the morning Mary Kris and I will wonder how the covers got so messed up.

The cat is back. I'm lying on my side, and I run in place like a sleeping dog chasing a rabbit. I finally get my feet out from under the covers and from under the cat. By scrunching the covers, I have now succeeded in quadrupling the thickness of covers on top of me. But my feet lie gasping in the cold night air, grateful to once again breathe the frigid January air of our bedroom.

* * *

"Cold" has taken a bad rap. Most everyone talks badly about "cold," but I have begun to appreciate the cold. Today we are trapped in hot houses, confined in over-heated cars, sausaged inside thermal underwear and ballooned parkas as a protection against what? Cold?

Things work better when they are a little cool, under the friendly bite of cold air. Aah, what a pleasure--the refreshing invigoration of a blast of winter.

When I was a kid milking cows or chopping wood on our dairy farm, I don't think I ever heard Dad complain about winter or any bad weather. Comment on it--always. Forecast it--frequently. Work in it--of course. But complain?--never.

If I were lamenting the snow, his song was, "Let it snow. Let it snow. Let it snow." When I'd complain about the rain, he'd sing "Rain--When you gonna rain again? Rain..." It was annoying.

Winter for Dad, was a time for fun. He'd spend all fall looking forward to and preparing for winter. When the first snow arrived, the horses would be harnessed and hitched to the sleigh. When winter arrived in earnest, he'd be out on the ice, fishing or skating. He worked outside seemingly oblivious to the cold I was complaining and shivering about. He'd only question, "What are you going to do when it gets cold?"

The coldest job on the farm was grinding feed for the cows. It required hours of standing next to the hammer mill and tending the gunny sacks being filled with corn and grain reduced to a course meal. The noise vibrated the cold into my fingers and toes. After hours of filling sacks I'd gain a layer of corn meal insulation as the dust settled on my eyelashes, hat and every other part of me. Once done, I could finally go into the warm. Pounding my limbs or stomping my feet, caused electrical shocks to course through my body as my near-frozen extremities thawed back to life.

Being a dairy farmer meant weather was never an excuse for not doing something. Every day, twice a day, the cows had to be tended--no excuses--no matter the weather. Of course weather was always a consideration. Depending on the weather you might do things differently. For example, you might dress differently, but you would still do it--no excuses.

The same unbendable philosophy toward weather influenced all parts of our lives. Bad weather was not an excuse for not doing, not visiting, not anything.

"Dad," I asked, as I pushed the fishing boat away from shore and hopped in. 'What do we do if it rains?"

"Let it rain," was his invariable reply.

"Ya, but what if we get wet?"

"We were born wet," was his inarguable response.

Of all of Dad's favorite seasons, I think winter was his best. For me, winter was my least favorite and waking in the dark and cold of January to milk a couple dozen dairy cows was hardest. Waking in the long days of summer was better. In the long summer days it was at least light, and the cows were clean and sleek. In the spring the predawn promised daylight and the songs of wrens and the chattering of the purple martins helped coax arousal.

But winter was hard. It was dark and cold, and I wanted to hibernate until spring under the thick pounds of wool quilts heaped on my bed in the unheated upstairs farmhouse. I'd huddle there in the dark delaying the transition from warm to the morning cold until I had no choice. The cows demanded milking and of course, the milking ritual was reinforced by Dad and my big brother Duane.

The challenge that long ago, dark, January 5 AM morning was how to get into my clothes without suffering the cold of the room. I crawled down under the blankets to the foot of the bed and stuck one bare arm out the side of the bed into the frigid air of my bedroom and groped the floor finding the rag rug, a shoe, then my shirt and pants. They were right where I had dropped them the night before. I pulled them under the covers and they came leaking polar wind into my warm cocoon. I pulled them on quickly hoping to escape the invading cold, but both pants and shirt were saturated with cold that quickly warmed to my body.

Having conquered the hardest step, I swung my feet out of bed and used my toes to find my shoes in the dark. My shoes were heavy leather, ankle high, work boots. I would have preferred the light canvas tennis shoes the town kids wore, but I was stuck with these unfashionable, but functional work shoes.

I laced them up and clomped downstairs. The house was freezing. My big brother Duane had probably added wood to the basement furnace on his way out to the barn, but as yet, the house was still cold. The heavy work shoes, cold and stiff, seemed to draw the last bit of warmth out of me as I made it to the kitchen and put on my wool Army surplus coat. That was cold also, draining more heat from my body. I had to get warm.

I turned on the electric oven and watched the coils that framed the bottom of the oven begin to glow in the still-dark kitchen. I adjusted the oven door so that I could drape my body over the oven. The heat was so weak I opened my coat like the wings of a hen on a clutch of eggs to capture all the oven's heat. Then I leaned over the partially open oven door, put my head on the top of the stove and went to sleep.

I woke up shortly with my mid-section uncomfortably hot and noticed the frayed edges of my wool coat were glowing. This was no good. My hands and feet were still cold and my chest was about to burst into flames. I brushed off the burning frays, shut off the oven, and resigned myself to the barn.

As kids, we complained about everything: Why is the farm so far from town? Why is the driveway so long? This morning it was: Why is the house so far from the barn? This I wondered and whined about as I buttoned up my coat, sealing in some of the heat from the oven. I donned hat and mittens, stopped on the porch to find my boots in the pile of twenty to forty boots the ten of us had for work and play and went outside.

It is deathly quiet at 5 AM on a frigid January morning in Minnesota. All critters with good sense have gone South or are burrowed deep under the snow waiting for spring. Even the animals that don't hibernate, like squirrels, will sleep for days until it warms up--of course then it will snow. Winter in Minnesota is balanced between bitter cold and warm-enough-to-snow. This morning it is bitter cold. It has been a week since the temperature was above zero. All our livestock are indoors and the snow crunches that twenty degree below zero crunch and I break into a run to get to the barn.

The first breath of cold bites my lungs, and I am careful to inhale only shallow breaths. My gait is peculiar to Minnesotans wearing too many layers of thick clothing. My arms are nearly straight. Neither elbows or knees have much room to bend. My feet are kept wide to keep the floppy-rubber-buckle-boots from hitting each other, catching, and landing me on my face. My steps are small, almost shuffles, to maintain balance across ice.

I unlatch the barn door and step through the milkhouse into the barn and am hit by the familiar smell of thirty cows and calves riding out the winter in very close quarters. It jolts me, but the shallow-breathing-running forces a deep catch-up breath, and I inhale deeply the warm moist air of the barn, warm air made moist by these gentle beasts; air that has condensed into window frost two inches thick. The air was like a tonic. Finally! Warmth! Moisture! It was a warm comfortable air that slipped deep into my lungs.

The barn was buttoned up as tight as we could make it and all that recirculated air must have been oxygen poor, because I was asleep on my floppy-rubber-buckle-boots. With the cold, the dark, the early hour and the seasonal demands of hibernation, I could barely make it to the first comfortable cow lying in her stall.

The cows were used to us. They didn't seem to mind if we slept on them. Occasionally, they would stand up when brother Dave came by with the silage, or Duane would wake them for their turn under the milker. If that happened, I'd slide off as she stood up and find another cow farther up the line.

It is best to be selective when choosing a cow. The best mikers are bone skinny. As Duane says, "They put the hay in the milk pail, not on their backs." Some of the cows were like sleeping on a pile of iron pipes. With a little selection and luck, you could find one who was currently not producing milk. They acquired a little padding on their bones while on a milking vacation, and they didn't have to be stood up to be milked which interrupted my sleep. Also, if they were big-bellied pregnant, it was like lying on a giant hot water bottle. That was the best.

Cow-snoozing is a seasonal activity, like skiing. You can't do it in the summer. It only works in the winter when the cows sleep indoors. In the summer they are all awake after their walk home from pasture. Sleeping on a standing cow was risky. It was tried, but to no avail. Sleeping under a standing cow was considered, but several cats demonstrated the dangers of that.

Well, Rusty is back from doing his rounds and has made sure the backyard is safe from squirrels. He waits at the sliding glass door staring at my empty dinner plate. He comes in covered with glitter-snow, which he immediately shakes off, leaving a three-foot splatter of snow becoming water that hits me from the knees down.

Aah cold. It is January. It is Minnesota. Things are the way they should be, but not to worry. In a couple months we'll be bragging (I mean complaining) about the heat. In the meantime it's dark; it's cold--I think I'll get the cat and go to bed.

The Swarm
(When You Lose Someone)

The Swarm
(When You Lose Someone)

I was sitting in church right between the large stained-glass windows of St. Peter the Rock and St. John the Baptist, listening to the music, and thinking about the lives this church has baptized and buried. I was busying my mind remembering everything that had happened there, hoping the jumbled thread of memories would distract me from Aunt Mary's funeral that I was attending.

The church held memories of: Baptisms, the purple shrouded statues of Lent, Good Friday stations, weddings, bringing flowers to the Virgin in May, the organ on Easter, and the sleepy scent of evergreen at midnight mass on Christmas eve. Father Milo, led by the altar boys, entered the church, and I remembered the dawn bicycle rides to church during the summer where I was the altar boy; reciting the Latin liturgy quickly, deftly; moving around the alter with practiced precise genuflections, anticipating the priest's every need.

The funeral service started, interrupting my remembering. The church was full for Aunt Mary's funeral. Lots of relatives showed up. The good-news-bad-news of living in a small town is that we are related to everyone. We always joked about this until we had a discovery reunion. Nearly everyone from town showed up because nearly everyone was somehow related. What I thought was a metaphor for how tightly everyone was involved in everyone else's life turned out to be genetically provable.

As I sat there, trying not to get emotionally involved in this funeral, a bee mistook the top of my head for an airport landing strip. This was only a small concern. I like bees. They won't harm you unless you threaten them.

Now if I had more hair the bee would have landed on my head like a kid on a haystack, bounced and flown off. If I had less hair, the bee could have taxied down the scalp runway and practiced touch-and-go landings all through the funeral. Instead the bee got snarled in the high-line wires of my hair and became as angry and frightened as a horse tangled in barbed wire.

I could hear her bee wings beating at full buzz as she tried to power her way through the tangle. I didn't want to swat at her to really make her angry. I rolled my eyes up into my head to watch her progress. Then she got tired and sat down to rest. Of course she sat down right on her stinger.

Ouch!

Time to leave. Not wanting squashed bee bodies on my headtop, I offered the top of my head to my brother Dave who gave flight instructions to the entangled bee, and I was left with a wounded scalp throbbing like a beacon on an airport runway.

Ow!

Years earlier, shortly after dad died, I was sitting at the kitchen table at the farm when a black cloud passed by the kitchen window. It was a cloud of honeybees that had swarmed to find a new home. As a kid, I had seen swarms float by as I spent long summer hours on the tractor cultivating corn. Swarms were slightly ominous events because of their infrequency and because their distraction usually resulted in the death of several yards of baby corn as I watched their flight instead of the cornrows.

What happens in the bee kingdom is that during a successful time the hive grows too big. To flourish it must divide, much like a cell, and reproduce. So the hive produces a second queen. This new queen takes half the hive on a mating flight. At the end of the flight she stops, mates with one of the thousand suitors, and builds a new home.

Here was a swarm of bees all anxiously wanting the virgin queen to stop this silly chase so they could get on with the mating ritual. She did. She stopped right outside the kitchen window on one of the upper branches of our white birch tree. The cloud trailing the queen congealed on the branch and became a crawling mass of bee-bodies. The late arrivals were sure there was a queen somewhere in this seething mass, but the early suitors hopelessly shielded them from the queen.

I had never seen a swarm land before. I had never done any beekeeping either, but I had watched Dad put on his beekeeper mask and clothes, start the burlap burning in his teapot shaped smoker, and work a hive.

The arrival of a fully-garbed beekeeper at a hive is like the beginning of a High Mass. The priest garbed in hat and robe would enter the sanctuary wearing the robes of High Mass, led by altar boys who handed him the required ritual tools that would please God and bring benefit to the parish family. The priest took the incense burner from the altar boy. I handed Dad the bee smoker and we stood shoulder-to-shoulder, our backs against the summer breeze. I dug in my pocket for the matches as Dad held out a piece of burlap for me to light. The altar boy offered the priest the bowl of incense. The priest scooped three spoonfuls of incense onto the burning coals in the bottom of the incense burner and the smoke rose in fragrant gray clouds. The burlap caught fire and Dad blew out the flame and stuffed the glowing threads into the bottom of the beekeeper smoker and began pumping the billows that blew on the smoking threads and kept the embers glowing and the smoke blowing. The priest respectfully approached the altar offering incense to all corners before ascending the steps of the altar. Dad began working the billows, generating a great cloud of smoke, moving upwind so that the smoke would flow to the hive. After bathing the hive in a general cloud of smoke, he approached the hive and began smoking the entrance in earnest. The priest having incensed the altar, as ritual demanded, handed the incenser to the altar boy, genuflected, and opened the tabernacle. Dad handed the smoker to me, picked up a flat iron and began prying off the top of the hive. The altar boy gently swung the incense burner, and absently watched the incense trail the burner penduluming first left, then right, keeping the fire burning in case another offering of incense was required. I played with the smoker trying to figure the mechanics of the smoke generation. Wondering why it didn't burst into flame or go out completely.

The priest began the ritual of communion. He removed the bread of life from the tabernacle, cleaned the utensils, and recited the required prayers. Dad pulled out one of the supers, a wood frame, that held the honeycomb. It was one third empty, one third with filled honeycombs, and one third with newly built but empty honeycombs waiting to collect the nectar from each bee. Dad described what he found.

"Can I see?" I asked from my safe and respectful distance. The priest turned and held up a host for the congregation to view. Dad turned to me and showed me the super. He was looking for a full super. It takes bees three times as much nectar to make beeswax as it does to make honey. Dad broke off a piece of honeycomb for me to chew. The altar boy knelt and accepted the host from the priest. Dad put the super back so the honeycomb could be filled. The priest turned back to the altar. Dad put the super back and continued cleaning and searching for a full super. The altar boy ascended the altar and held the great red leather-bound bible so the priest could read. Dad handed me the flat iron and called me to come up by him. He pulled up the hive nursery. It still held many of the nurses in addition to the baby bees in every stage of development. The nurses seemed oblivious to our presence. They continued to clean and tend and feed the blind pupas. Dad had removed the super only part way. He held it there and pointed out a larva ready to become a bee and a new bee just leaving its cone. "Where's the queen?" I whispered.

"Laying eggs in another part of the hive."

"Why isn't she taking care of her babies?"

"Not her job. She only lays the eggs. The worker bees take care of the babies."

Satisfied that all was well, he finished his quick inspection, and replaced the nursery. He broke apart all supers from each other, inspected some other supers and closed up the hive. The priest returned the sacred contents back into the tabernacle.

We left the altar.

Now, years later, there was a brand new swarm looking for a home, just twenty feet up into a birch tree. What to do?

I called up the family lawyer and fellow beekeeper.

"How do you capture a swarm?" I asked after describing the circumstance.

Having read one too many law books the lawyer-beekeeper said, "You offer the queen a super from the nursery. She will be attracted by the hatch. The swarm will follow."

"Well, how do I get the nursery out of an existing hive? It's going to be guarded by bees."

"What you do is: snip a sprig from a convenient bush, gingerly whisk the attending bees off the nursery, and spirit the super away."

"Thanks," I said hanging up the phone.

Bees might allow you to pillage their hives for a little honey, but I figured they would be less accommodating when it came to stealing their babies.

I went to the garage and found Dad's beekeeper gloves, coveralls and rubber binders to seal up all clothing orifices, better known as bee entrances. And, of course, I found the beekeeper's straw hat complete with veil. I put everything on, surprised that everything fit. I always thought Dad was much bigger than I was.

The smoker was already loaded with burlap. The pockets had wood matches. I got a saw and an extension ladder from the tool shop and deposited everything under the swarm, now thirty inches long and ten inches thick, a solid mass of bees.

First, I had to kidnap bee babies. I fired up the smoker, snipped a sprig, gingerly whisked, and spirited away (in a very spirited fashion) and put the stolen nursery in an empty hive.

Now there was the logistics problem of how to get the swarm to the prepared nursery? I stretched the extension ladder to its full length, leaned it on the flimsy branches of the outer crown of the birch tree and began climbing with a saw in one hand, the smoker in the other.

The bees ignored me completely.

It is interesting to see the fine details of a bee body. It is fascinating to see their handiwork of honeycomb and watch them work, but it is nearly indescribable to approach a swarm of thousands of bees, to cut that mass of life out of a tree and carry it to a new home. With the branch, the swarm weighed about ten pounds. Throughout this process I never feared the bees or feared for my life. Killer bees were still in Africa. They hadn't become a news item yet. I was more fascinated with the privilege of capturing the hive than the common sense of fearing for my life.

I expected that at any moment the queen would fly off, continue her mating flight and leave me holding an empty birch branch. Instead, I laid the swarm on top of the hive holding the stolen nursery and stepped back. Now nature would have to take its course. Certainly one of these many thousand bee suitors would be to the queen's liking; they would mate, and we could get on with the business of hive building.

Everything happened as the bee lawyer predicted. I came back later, removed the branch and buttoned up the hive. Everyone seemed happy with their new home.

I called the lawyer-beekeeper. I told him about my success and told him that there were dozens of bees still circling where the swarm had landed. He said they were lost scouts. They would never be able to find the swarm. He said they would continue to circle at the swarm's last location until they died.

I felt bad for the lost bees. He said the hive would be OK without them.

I remembered all this as I rubbed my wounded scalp and sat-stood-knelt through Aunt Mary's funeral. And I wondered that since our family, our hive, is so big, you would think that an absent face would not be so sorely missed. Fortunately, there is great comfort in a large family and a well-attended funeral. It reaffirms that we are not alone and have not been diminished by the loss of one of our own. Simultaneously, the loss is more poignant, the grief more present, and the sense of separation more permanent when it is a part of family, a part of ourselves that dies.

We can take solace in the lawyer-beekeeper's words. We will be "OK" when we lose one of ourselves, because we are protected, cared for, and loved by God and each other.

Silent Secrets
(The Value of Nothing).

Silent Secrets
(The Value of Nothing)

Growing up in a houseful of siblings and the constant din of our togetherness meant we were never lonely. Nevertheless, despite the ten of us crammed into the country farmhouse, quiet or solitude was only a step away. At any time I could walk directly away from the noise and find a shaggy-barked hickory tree under which to puzzle the nuts back into their husks. Or enjoy the rustling quiet of the cornfield, as the gunslinger cornstalks, an ear of corn strapped on each hip, marched by in tidy rows that curved gently around the hill. Or there was the peaceful quiet of the haymow, offering a perch on top the summer's harvest, or hiding a dusty hay-cave built deep within the mountain of bales. Or, I could climb onto a roof. There I was lifted above the world, above any worries. There I had a different perspective, and peace, and privacy. Roofs were silent secrets abandoned by adults.

My first favorite roof was the old chicken coop. It was my favorite because it was the first one I could climb. It was a long, low, narrow coop with the traditional 14" wide barn wood siding. It had been painted red many years earlier, but time had reduced the paint to a red oxidized powder. The roof was cedar shingles, turned soft with age and edged with green moss.

My initial discovery of the roof was not in search of silence, but the lucky discovery of a youth in search of everything. Climbing over the half-height barn door accessed the roof. From there I could reach the underside of the roof. A short stretch, a leg up and I scrambled to a view overlooking orchards and fields.

There is nothing more contemplative then lying on a roof watching clouds on a sun-scrubbed summer's day. There I spent careless youthful days when my greatest concern was how to keep from sliding off because sitting on the very peak of the roof quickly became uncomfortable. I was more comfortable lying spread-eagled on my back near the top of the roof with my hands holding onto the peak of the roof. It was a nice position and gave me the feeling that I was hanging above the earth.

Once while in that position I discovered my second most favorite position when I slipped and slid down the roof until a shingle nail caught me by the seat of my pants. Aside from giving me a wedgie, I had both hands free to do important things like: counting my fingers, having a thumb war with myself, or picking at the moss edges of the shingles. Best though, was the contemplative opportunity for silence uninterrupted by the need to hang on or carry on a conversation. The silence was nice. In a houseful of siblings I could be alone there on the roof.

My second favorite roof was the old-old calf barn. Even in my youth the building was nearly gone. It had neither doors nor glass in its windows, but it had a nearly flat roof. I found that by standing on the top board of the hogyard fence, I could reach the roof and scramble up. It was sufficiently difficult that my younger brothers couldn't get up without my help. That turned the roof into my private sanctuary where I watched the barn swallows, pigeons, pigs and cows all enjoy the farm. It was my place of silence; a place where I learned to watch. A roof is a unique place because it sets you apart from life. The rest of the world goes on around you, but you can't participate. You can't bring things onto the roof because they roll off. While you're on the roof your role is observer. Cows, birds or brothers might come right up to the edge of your observation, but they were worlds away. I had very distinct times when I was a participant (off the roof) and when I was an observer (on the roof).

It was on the roof and perhaps in church that I learned to keep my mouth shut and enjoy the silence. Silence earmarked the important times on the farm which was usually a noisy place. Dad first pointed out to me the role silence played in our family one winter when the two of us were standing on the Mississippi. I was a little kid. Dad was helping me extract my foot and boot from a fishing hole he had chopped in the ice. My boot went down in the hole easily enough, but it didn't want to come up with my foot. I stood there on the green river ice with my wet pants cuff freezing into ankle armor while Dad reached down into the hole and retrieved my floppy-rubber-buckle boot.

Dad didn't say, "That was a stupid thing to do." When he was on the river, nothing could go wrong. After Dad poured the river water out of my boot and stuck it upside down on a stick to drain and dry, I sat on his lap and he told me for the first time how he and his brother Julius would drive the team of horses and sled down into the valley to Scheck's millpond on Beaver Creek and harvest blocks of ice.

It was January in the 1930's. They were on the big millpond created by the dam built to provide waterpower for Scheck's Mill. They had the great two-man saw used to saw the crystal clear spring water into ten-pound ice blocks. Dad jokingly complained that since he was the younger brother, he always got stuck with the handle under water. They also had the great ice tongs used to drag the blocks out of the water. The ice was to be sledded home and packed in sawdust until needed in July or August to cool the milk or to make ice cream.

That frigid winter day Julius was standing at the edge of the ice using the great tongs to pull the blocks out of the icy water when he slipped and fell into the water.

Julius grabbed the edge of the ice and pulled himself out and rolled back onto the ice, got up and started running. He never said a word. He just headed for home. Dad untied the team of horses and turned the sled around and headed out after him. He caught up with Julius about a mile away where the road turned upward, and twisted and turned its way up the side of the bluff. Julius was breathing hard but making good time. His clothes had turned stiff and frozen solid around him, but he continued running. My Dad said nothing either. He drove the team and kept pace with Julius who ran as if his life depended on it.

This silence is a trait I've noticed in the men in my family. When there's trouble, no sense talking about it--fix it. I always knew when something was serious. If something was trivial, there might be lots of noise, but if it was serious it would get real quiet.

Quiet didn't always indicate imminent disaster. Quiet came to the farm every day as regular as prayer. I was reminded of this on my last sleepover at the farm. Sometime in the small morning hours, my eyes opened into darkness. Sleep was totally pushed away. There was a roar, a constant white-noise roar. What was its source?

My eyes bumped around in the blackness searching for a point of reference, some focal point. Where was I? There--a dresser--a door. I was visiting at the farm, tucked safely in an upstairs bedroom.

The roar was the familiar sound of quiet caused by sensory deprivation--complete quiet. After years of living in the constant din of the city the roar of silence was a jolt. I listened to the silence, the roar of white-noise in my ears, and wondered what caused it. Was it caused by blood rushing past the eardrum? Was it the result of an ear canal empty of sound waves? The emptiness allowing random, unorganized, ambient energies to bang against my eardrum?

The roar was deafening. I rolled over to face the window that allowed the moon to reveal the door and dresser to me. Rolling over caused some very satisfying creaks and squeaks from the old box spring. The roar stopped as the clean sheets scraped noisily against my skin, and I paused mid-roll and fingered the edge of the sheet. Aah sound! I haven't gone deaf. I continued my rollover toward the moonlit window. The bed's ancient box spring complained, and I exaggerated the rollover to generate more happy sounds and drive the silence out of my ears. My rollover complete, I lay there in silence, watching the rolling countryside, listening to nothing, and slipped into a peaceful soundless sleep until morning arrived.

Many years ago the old-old calf barn collapsed under the winter snows. I didn't mind. I had grown a bit and become a master of the farm's roofs. There were the tin roofs of the shop and machine shed, the tar roofs of the brooder house chicken coop, the asphalt shingles of the corncrib, and the cedar shakes of the farmhouse, barn, slop house and hog house. Each offered a different view of the world. I soon discovered that I was fascinated with heights and the windmill. The metal frame of the windmill was scanty enough to give me the sensation that I was suspended in mid-air. As the clouds rushed by overhead, I was certain I was moving or that the windmill was tipping over. Perhaps that sensation was prophetic because younger brother Dave ran a tractor into the windmill and toppled it like a great oak.

With the windmill gone, the silo offered an interesting vantage point. The ladder bolted to its side only went to the top of the cylindrical part of the silo. When I ran out of ladder at the top, I had to shimmy up the curved dome of the silo using only the friction of the palms of my hands. At the very top was a manhole. It was open. The silo was empty. I stuck my head in and yelled down into the hollowness, enjoying the echo. That was always one of the treats we'd offer the townies when they came to visit--we'd let them yell into the silo to hear their own echo.

What a great vantage point. I was at the top of the world. I could see everything--well, almost everything. The barn blocked my vision to the West. So I stood up. Cool. Now I could see forever.

I stood there with one foot on either side of the open manhole with the fearlessness that only the very young have, raised both hands over my head, and reached up to touch the sky. Then I made the big mistake--I looked up. The sky was moving. Clouds were sailing past. It gave me the sensation I was moving and that the silo was tipping. I flinched and went into an immediate squat right into the open manhole. I fell. As I fell, my arms came down from over my head and slapped onto the dome on either side of the manhole stopping my fall. I hung by my armpits for a second with my feet kicking at emptiness before I pulled myself back onto the silo roof. Now I wanted "down."

I slid over to the ladder and found that I was too short to reach it. It was just beyond the curved top of the silo, out of sight. I would have to let go of the manhole and slide blind, off the roof and hope I landed on the top of the ladder. It was only a drop of a couple feet, but I couldn't see that. When you're suspended 35 feet above the ground after nearly falling, letting go is difficult. My aim was fine. I landed on the ladder. My knees were shaking as I descended the ladder to the ground.

I went somewhere and was very quiet.

It's interesting that quiet, or silence, is a state of nothingness. Silence is a concept or a symbol for something that really doesn't exist. Noise or sound is vibration. It is something. Silence is our term for when there is no vibrational energy. Silence, which is nothingness, doesn't exist. It is essentially no sound. Like so many things in our world we think that if we have a name for something we know it; we understand it. We have given the name "silence" to "nothing" and declared it something.

Nothing, or things that don't exist, are quite acceptable for us. For example, take our concepts of "light" and "dark." We understand both terms. "Light" is energy. "Dark" is the absence of "light." Dark does not exist. It is nothing. Dark is only definable by describing what is not there. Yet so much of our society and our language is based on this non-existence "dark."

We require what does not exist. We require dark. If everything were pure light, there would be no gradations in what we see. Everything would be one constant purity of brilliance. So we have introduced degrees of non-existence, darkness, to delimit the presence of light. Without darkness we would have no physical vision. Since darkness does not exist (it being the absence of light), we base our entire perception, indeed our entire vision of the world, on something that does not exist--nothing.

Back on my long ago roofs I discovered the treasure of nothing--of rooftop quiet. I didn't know what I had. Then I thought that Life valued what could be seen, heard, or touched. Now I know that the important stuff is what cannot be seen, heard or touched. That includes our perceptions, our experiences and our memories. And let's not forget the angels that followed me across the roofs, the love we shared as family, and of course the all-encompassing spirit of God that cares so clearly for each of us. None of these things "exist" in the physical sense, yet they define who we are, and what we value.

We require nothing (no thing). We the souls; we the spirit living inside these bodies need no thing. It is when we pause in the silence, or dark, or in the space between breaths that we notice the nothingness that defines this world.

While we live in this world we occasionally require a little nothing, a little quiet in our minds. Eventually that quiet requires something: talking; doing; writing and in every case sharing. It is this sharing of our thoughts, our abilities, and ourselves that gives us the peace and the joy in our lives. After all, what would rest be if not earned? ...Endless boredom. What would quiet be without interruption? ...Intolerable solitude. What would family be without friendship? ...Don't know??? Certainly not what I've experienced.

Well, I've gone on and on about nothing. As we sang in church on Sunday:

"I've got nothing in my pocket and I don't feel bad.

Nothing in the bank and I don't feel sad.

I've got more treasure than a millionaire.

All I need is heaven and he's taking me there."

There's nothing like a little nothing to remind us how much we have.

The Clothesline
(Remember Who You Are)

The Clothesline
(Remember Who You Are)

Our clothes dryer broke today. It was a breakdown of some consequence. It broke down just when I wanted to use it. There I was with an armful of wet wash and no dryer. Fortunately I grew up during an era when the sun and wind were our clothes dryer. Then the great outdoors did the work of this broken machine. So I set out to dry my clothes the old-fashioned way--outdoors.

I carried my one load of wash out of the basement and onto the deck where I remembered I was missing a few things--like a clothesline. We do have one end of a clothesline. We have one of the posts, a "T" built out of two-inch water pipes still standing in the backyard, but no "line."

As a kid, I hung out with Mom as she hung wash on the clothesline. Sheets were my favorite. Mom would occasionally use the clothesline and the sheets to build me a sunlight-filled tent where I played my child's games until the sheets dried and Mom folded my tent into squares and placed them on neat piles where they waited their rotation onto the beds. It was not without some fuss that I relinquished my claim on her clothesline tent. And, not to be denied, I once stole a sheet off of her neat shelves and built my own tent. I was too small to clothespin the sheets to the clothesline, so I used the picket fence as a lean-to. The pickets made nice holes in the sheet to keep it from falling down. The bottom was held in place by pounding screwdrivers through the sheet as tent stakes. That was where I made the vital mistake. If I had just destroyed the sheet, Mom and I would have worked things out, but no, I had to bring Dad's tools (and Dad) into my inventiveness.

They both talked to me.

But, what am I to do today? One end of a clothesline is about as useful as one hand clapping. When Mom ran out of clothesline, the smaller things like handkerchiefs and socks would be sprinkled on the grass to dry. So I scattered my wet stuff around the deck.

When I started helping Mom with the wash, we had a washhouse--an entire out-building set aside for laundry.   Unfortunately that washhouse didn't have hot water or even running water. It did have the great washtubs Mom used to scrub the clothes. Right outside was a deep cistern and a long-handled pump that provided the soft water rainwater collected off the cedar shake roof of our farm home. Mom heated the rainwater and carried it into the washhouse. For laundry detergent, Mom and my sister Alice made lye soap out of the ashes from the furnace, hog drippings and other toxic stuff. The great wood-fired slop cauldron in the hog house was used to heat the caustic brew. When it cooled, the lye was cut into brick-sized bricks. Our house was not kid-proof or kid-safe. We had loaded guns within an easy climb, but these lye bricks were dangerous enough to be stored on the top-most shelf to keep them from inquisitive toddlers. At wash time, Mom would heat up one of the bricks on the wood-fired stove and add the melted lye to a load of wash.

Back when Mom was a young wife there wasn't that much laundry. There was just me, my big brother and sister, Dad and the hired help or two. Back then, we didn't change clothes every day like the compulsive peacocks of today. We waited until the Saturday bath. Then maybe, maybe it was time for a clean set of clothes. Of course, it didn't matter much anyway. All clothes looked the same. The "clean" I put on, was pretty much the same as the "dirty" I took off. Between changes my clothes seemed to shape themselves to my body. It was easy to tell which sock belonged on my right foot and which on my left. My work pants had preformed bends at the knees, and my pockets held everything I needed because I had stocked them the previous day. Mom knew that I kept my treasures in my pockets, so I didn't understand all the screaming when she found a garter snake in my jeans.

My siblings and I were just getting off the school bus when the screaming started. The lane to our farm was really long, so it was really good screaming for us to hear Mom that far away. We ran up the lane to find her looking ashen, and leaning on a wall in the hallway outside my bedroom. I got my first taste of super-hero rescue work by saving Mom and returning my snake, Greenie, to his outdoor home. I think the screaming upset Greenie because when I sat him down he seemed real glad to get back to doing snake things, and he forgot all about being my pet. I didn't really want to let him go, but Mom seemed to be able to make complete sentences after I carried him outside.

I complained to Dad about the length of our lane. Not that it was unusual for me to be complaining about something. I asked Dad why we had such a long lane? He said it was to keep the wash hanging on the clothesline clean. The dust that trailed the cars and tractors traveling the gravel road that ran in front of our farm would settle back to earth before it could make it to the clothesline.

Dad also suggested I not leave snakes in the laundry. He said, No, he didn't understand why women and girls didn't like snakes, but he said there were a lot of things about women he'd never understand.

Fortunately, things were relatively easy when I was small. First, I didn't have to do them. Second, there were only the few of us. The rest of the family hadn't been born. I was still the youngest. Later, John, Dave, Mark, Rita and Jane would show up in rapid succession. Then the laundry skyrocketed. Attitudes changed. People started bathing mid-week and expected to put on clean clothes.

Mom scrambled to keep ahead of the avalanche of dirty laundry. The washtubs were upgraded to a washing machine with a hand wringer, but we still carried water. I use the inclusive term "we" because I sometimes tagged along.

To help Mom keep ahead of the laundry, we (again the inclusive "we") built a laundry room in the basement complete with running water (hot and cold), put down a cement floor, and grandma Josey gave Mom a real washing machine--one with a powered clothes ringer. Sure we still had to manually drain and fill the tubs but it was almost automatic--easy.

The good-news-bad-news of moving the washing into the basement with hot and cold running water and a town-fancy wringer washing machine was that now the wash had to be carried load, after load, after wet-heavy load, up the stairs and around to the east side of the house where Dad had sunk the posts for the clothesline. I think Dad knew way back in the beginning that he was going to have a house full of kids because he didn't build the wimpy, one-post, T-type clothesline like the one abandoned in my backyard. Dad sunk two-legged four-inch pipes deep into the ground and anchored them with cement. He sunk them so deep that Mom could hang a ton of laundry without even straining them. They still stand like two monster bookends without books but with a story to tell.

These two obelisks that served as the defining points of our clothesline observed the unfolding of our family history. They noticed the birth of the first child and proudly held up his diapers for the neighbors to see. They watched as the clothes grew in size and flagged the work shirts. They watched me play under the lines as Mom hung socks and shirts pushing the clothespin bag ahead of her. Diapers would regularly appear as more and more kids were born into our family. They noticed when holidays came and the best table linens were washed. They knew when company stayed over and our special bedding took its turn in the sun.

Nearly every family event was recorded on those clotheslines: Uniforms from Army, Navy and Air Force decorated the lines, as did my sister's poodle skirts hanging in perfect half-circles. They held up wedding dresses, the First Communion whites in the spring, 4-H whites at fair time, and homecoming dresses in the fall. They knew when Mom finished a big batch of fresh-baked bread and a new, flowered flour sack joined the wash as a pillowcase.

They watched when Mom and Dad had a car accident and brother Mark was born prematurely. Then the laundry was hung in a different order as older cousins helped keep us in clean clothes. Everything our family did, and every time our family grew, it was advertised to the passing neighbors by the clothesline.

After Dad started a tar fire on the kitchen stove, mom finally got an automatic washer and dryer installed in the pantry off the kitchen. The unused clothesline still stands just outside the pantry window. It waits. It knows that some day the dryer will break down. It waits. It's ready. As long as the sun shines and the wind blows, it is ready to note the events of its family. Until then it waits on the east side, on the sunrise side of life, content that when Mom checks the morning sun and notes the diamond dew sprinkled on the grass, or catches the moonrise on an autumn night, or wonders at the winter-blue snowdrifts sculpted over the sleeping garden, it waits, content that she view all this through its pillared arms that frames her scenery through every season.

It has now been a month since our dryer broke. It has taken us that long to admit the dryer was dead, decide to buy a new one, find one for a reasonable price, and wait and wait for it to be delivered.

Finally! The delivery guys are here with the new dryer. Two guys arrive with the dryer slung in a hammock between them. Zip-zip-zip the new dryer is delivered downstairs; the old one is slung in their shoulder hammock, and they're gone in minutes.

I went down and looked at the dryer sitting in the middle of the laundry room. (The delivery guys don't do hookups.) I checked it out. It seemed the make, model, size, and color we'd ordered. But I wondered if it was up to the job, up to my expectations. I planned on it being here a long time. It, too, would be involved in our continuing family history. I expect this new dryer to note the visits of company, the return of kids from college, the future visits of grandchildren, and the clothing changes of the seasons. The whole activity of our family will pass in and out of its care.

I slid it into place. I hooked it up and tossed the first load of family history into its yawning mouth. I slammed the door, played with all its knobs and selected one of its 87 cycles.

Thirty minutes later it began buzzing at me, demanding I remove and sort and fold this week's history. I removed my underwear and socks from the dryer, glad they were not flagging on a clothesline in the backyard for the neighbors to judge.

I can do without clotheslines (now that I have my dryer back). But when I want to remember, when I take a break from the work-a-day world and join my family for a weekend of remembering, we bring out all the things we no longer need: the campfire (we have our furnaces), the tent (we have our homes) and, of course, the clothesline. Just for remembering, I'm going to keep my one-ended, one-post clothesline in my backyard. It will help me remember my roots. It will help me remember who I am.

The Orange Prince
(A Second Chance)

The Orange Prince
(A Second Chance)

Unfortunately (or luckily) life continually provides memory joggers, or events or incidents that keep stirring the pot and keep reminding us of who we are and where we've come from. Some memories keep coming back insisting that I learn from them and usually I refuse, but luckily life often gives us a second chance.

When I was twelve, our dairy farm had cats. We had cats everywhere. They were all sizes, all colors, all attitudes--too many cats. These farm cats hired to keep the rodents at bay had themselves become a nuisance. Our farm was then picked clean of rodents and still the cats ranged across the fields and through the woods hunting and stalking.

These were working cats. These were no domesticated house pets that mewed gently for a second helping of salmon. These cats were uncuddled, unkempt and earned their food, but nevertheless, they were tied to our milking parlor like frogs to a pond. The twice-a-day milking drew them back to the barn as regular as the sun. The hu-chu... hu-chu... hu-chu... of the milking machines and the drone of the vacuum pump drew them from the field and hayloft, tree branches and crawl spaces, to sit impatiently in rings around us as we milked our way from one end of the barn to the other.

The cats were usually fed the milk from the last cow. After all the saleable milk was stripped from the cows, we'd then milk the cows just freshly calved. Their milk was too rich for sale; too full of the life that newborn calves needed. Sometimes the last milk was from an injured cow; where the milk, enriched by bossy's own blood, flowed pink as a foaming strawberry milk shake.

Pink milk wasn't as uncommon as you might think. Our cows, bred only for milk production, carried huge bags of milk that swung like pendulums when they walked and got under foot when they lay down. Literally under foot so that they'd step on themselves when they stood up.

When horses stand up, they get up on their front feet first, and then they get their back feet under themselves. Horses get up headfirst. Horses are runners and would just as soon sleep standing up. They seldom lie down. Their only reason for lying down is a good back-scratching roll in the dirt.

Cows do the opposite. They get their hind legs under themselves first, then their front feet. Cows get up butt first, but then cows are cud-chewers. They go out and mow the fields then head for a shady afternoon of lying down and chewing. Cows have made lying down an art and a life's ambition. The problem is that Mother Nature never intended cows to feed more than their own offspring and never intended them to carry such large burdens of milk. Generations of breeding have changed Mother Nature's design for cows. That change, coupled with the bovines' butt-first stand-up technique, is what allows them to step on themselves.

Cats, on the other hand, are hunters and stalkers. When they get up, the trunk of their body remains level. In the course of a stalking they may get up and down dozens of times; gently, quietly, smoothly; their legs folding and unfolding, the pads of their paws always on the ground, always at the ready.

And stalk us they did in this barn full of far too many cats. As we milked, the rings of cats adjusted itself to mirror our progress from cow to cow. The inside ring held the youngest and most domesticated cats and also the poorest hunters. They whined and begged from the first cow to the last, and they knew when their time had come. Then their mewing crescendoed and the ring of cats tightened into a circular sea of pussies jockeying for position around the cattle-feed dish turned giant milk saucer. My boots disappeared under the waves of cats leaning on my knees waiting for the milk. Then I'd pour and the whining stopped instantly. Those leaning on my knees would lap at the stream of still-airborne milk. The others standing shoulder-to-shoulder would lap from the lake of milk appearing before them.

Much of nature is secreted in a gentle whisper never intended for you to hear, but occasionally, like the hot July night my Dad woke me to hear the corn grow; or the time the inch-worms invaded town and I could sit under a tree and hear worms chew leaves; or when the fish flies were so thick I could hear them walk over each other and they enlisted snow plows in June to clear the bridges over the Mississippi; now I could hear the tiny sound of a kitten lapping milk as it was amplified by dozens of sandpaper tongues lapping the shore of a frothy sea of milk.

Cats are a curious crowd. Dogs have a pecking order of who is to eat first, and there is the growling and biting to enforce their hierarchy. Cats, by contrast, are like one large family. Shoulder-to-shoulder, needing only room to get their head in the dish, they lapped up the milk with eyes closed in satisfaction.

All the cats except one. All the cats except a big, beautiful, orange tiger cat. This cat would never accept a free handout or luxuriate in fresh, warm, raw milk. He would show up but never participate. When the rings of cats collapsed into a lapping frenzy, he'd watch from his perch, eyes fixed, tail alive.

I tried to befriend this prince of cats. I even delivered him his own saucer of milk set squarely in front of him only to have him back sideways away. He would not be bribed into dependence.

Then one day I found the Orange Prince within reach. He was napping on top of the cement wall that ringed the horse stalls. I reached out and petted him. He opened his eyes and glared at me unmoving. I petted him again and without remorse or fear, he bit me--hard. Pain, unique to punctures, paralyzed my hand. I shouted and shook my wounded paw.

The Orange Prince unhurriedly moved to the back of the wall, out of reach. I was annoying him. Perhaps if he put some little distance between himself and this squawking, wing-flapping, disturber of naps, he could return to important thoughts of fat mice and supple felines.

Blood oozed from my wound. Not a lot, but all of it mine. Stunned, my mind raced and dragged simultaneously. When your life is threatened, your life supposedly passes in front of you and its purpose and meaning achieve clarity. When your pride is threatened, every piece of data related to the threat pops to the surface of your conscious mind like swamp gas bubbles in a summer pond. Many times I've mistaken swamp gas for life's meaning and purpose. This, unfortunately, was one of those times.

I stood there, quieter now, squeezing the blood out of the puncture. Squeezing made it feel better, and the gradual accumulation of blood helped me feel "wronged." The more blood, the greater the wrong. I had been attacked--viciously. Mauled by...was the cat rabid? I had heard stories about rabid skunks and bats. *The swamp gas bubbled.* One of my classmates told about a cow that became rabid and slobbering and had to be put down. *More swamp gas.* I had just seen the movie "Ol Yeller" and saw how a loyal, trusted, family dog, bitten by a bear, went crazy and had to be destroyed.

I looked at the Orange Prince. No, I looked at this wild, mangy tomcat. Was he foaming at the mouth? *Swamp gas bubbled.* Animals have an innate fear and respect for humans. The Bible has granted man dominion over all animals. *Swamp gas boiled.* Only a rabid-crazy cat would attack a human a hundred times its size. My Dad's chest bore scars, witness to the insanity of an infected bobcat, or was it a raccoon?

The cat was rabid and needed...No, deserved what was coming. I'm sure I saw foam. One bad apple can spoil the barrel. I have to save the farm.

Swamp gas.

How to kill a cat? Not an easy decision. Twelve-year-old boys are always looking for an excuse to use a gun, but the cat was inside the barn. It would have made a mess. I walked to the shop. How to do it? There were lots of possibilities in the shop: there was a long handled three-foot scythe for harvesting grain--too clumsy; machetes for cutting corn stalks--too messy; meat hooks from the smoke house--not accurate; dynamite for blowing up stumps. Perfect! Catch the cat. Tie three sticks of dynamite to his back. Light the fuse-- and then what? Let the cat run into the barn? Besides there was the problem of "catching the cat."

There were more possibilities such as: burlap feed sacks. Catch the cat, put him in the sack and throw it into the pond. There was that "catch the cat" problem again. Gopher traps. were not big enough. Fox traps were not quick enough. The arc welder was a possibility. Put a clamp on his tail, crank up the juice and have cat meltdown. Never mind, I'd have to catch the cat. I saw more tools: Saws, hammers, hatchets and a hammer. Hammer! Blunt! Accurate! No blood!

My Dad had a wonderful, leather-handled, claw hammer that had survived all us kids. We liked nothing better than playing with Dad's tools. We built a birdhouse that would never house birds, airplanes out of two-by-fours, swords out of laths, and bows and arrows out of willows. The shop was filled with alchemist magic. We dragged tools and raw materials to the far reaches of the farm to build the weapons and forts of childhood fantasy. My Dad claimed there were tools buried everywhere; and he was right, but his hammer survived.

Back then this hammer's only flaw was an angular crease across the hammer's leather handle where a steel-wheeled steam engine had run over it. Years later its smooth steel would be black and pitted from spending a winter under the snow and the leather would be dry and rough, but it always returned. It survived, not like this darn cat that set out to spoil my day.

Ever noticed that people must change their attitude or opinion about the enemy before they can do them in? Loving mates must discover the other is a jerk and decide to divorce. Employers discover a trusted employee has become a gold brick. Friendly, helpful neighbors become the best of enemies. Countries declare only "just wars" against terrorists. An Orange Prince becomes a "darn cat." And why? We are creations with powerful imaginations. We can change a broken table into a treasured heirloom or into trash. And we can do the same with everything in our lives. Treasure it or trash it. At every moment we have the opportunity to contribute or to consume, to grow or to diminish, to love or to hate. We don't always make the right decision. Sometimes we have to open all the doors just to see and understand the difference.

I'm not happy about the events that day and how the alchemist's hammer in the hands of an apprentice took the life of the Orange Prince. I told my Dad about it. He listened. He said, "It probably needed to be done," which made me feel better. But I missed the Orange Prince's attendance at the milkings, and shortly after that all the cats disappeared. A virus swept through the farm and every cat died. We went out and recruited more cats, and they quickly died. For years, the farm was radioactive deadly for cats. Without the Orange Prince, it seemed no cat could live there.

But you know, the wonderful thing about life is you often get a second chance.

My daughter Miki had a cat despite my protests. She named her cat "Angus." Angus was a friendly gray and white bundle of kitten energy that chased string and shadows. She grew and gave Miki several litters of kittens, all of which were tolerated or ignored by me even though my kids loved them so.

Years later Miki was grown and moved out of home. Angus was old and sick and it was time for me to remember the Orange Prince forgotten for thirty years. I took Angus, alert but calm, wrapped in her blanket with only her head showing. Eyes wide and questioning. Ears alert. She rode in my lap as I drove alone to the vet. I held her in my arms as the vet, sympathetic but professional, injected the sleeping potion. Angus flinched from the needle, looked at me, and her bright yellow eyes turned black. It was as though a switch had been flipped, and the lights were turned out. Angus left to go where good cats go, and I was left holding a dead cat and all the memories of the Orange Prince.

The vet left me alone with my cat and my memories as I wept. Angry that I couldn't stop, and sad that I couldn't undo. A long time later they needed the examination room. They took the dead cat out of my arms, and I left. I left hot and soggy from the emotion, and I left both Angus and the Orange Prince there. I left them to rest. Somewhere in there I took the opportunity to forgive the Orange Prince; no, to forgive myself for what I did to him. And I discovered that forgiveness is always something you give yourself. I know that Mom and Dad and God and my siblings will always love me no matter how stupid I may occasionally act, and I learned in there that since we are all one, to condemn another is to condemn ourselves. Since the condemnation comes from ourselves, forgiveness, true forgiveness, comes from the removal of our self-imposed sentence and a return to our natural state, which is love.

We all look for opportunities to love, and the wonderful thing about life (have I said that before?)--the wonderful thing about life is I have another opportunity. I now live with another cat. She's a friendly, gray tiger cat that sits on my chest and purrs in my face. She doesn't do tricks, but she loves saucers of milk, short naps and bird watching. This cat seems insatiable for attention and relishes a good brushing and prolonged petting. It's as though this cat is intent on making up for my thirty years of cat neglect.

Thank goodness for second chances.

The Nose Knot
(Differences)

The Nose Knot
(Differences)

My wife Mary Kris and I went to a restaurant the other night. It was our weekly Thursday night out. One of those few nights when our schedules sync, and we get to spend some time with each other.

Our waitress was a young lady in her early twenties or late teens. Then again she could have been somewhere between twenty and fifty. It seems impossible to determine someone's age these days. Everyone is dyed and painted. The men plot against baldness, the women argue with gravity, and kids try to look older. Everyone is trying to look the same--just different within the sameness.

Our waitress delivered our menus and left quickly. Out of the corner of my eye I noticed she had something hanging from her nose. I ignored it (kind of), and began looking for something pronounceable on the menu.

I had my nose in the menu when she returned and had narrowed my menu choices down to seven items. I declared that I was ready to order and began a frantic eni-meani-mini-mo while Mary Kris ordered.

Then I saw it again. Something was definitely hanging off her nose. This time it glinted like it was wet. I tried not to look.

Now it was my turn to order. Because of the nasal distraction I had only made it a third of the way through my eni-meani. The waitress waited. Finally pleading, "What would you like to order?"

I was so embarrassed for her. It couldn't be good for tips. Maybe I should just say something, like: "Excuse me. Dad always told me, 'Son, to get ahead in life you have to keep your nose clean.'" That should be indirect enough. But she needed to figure out what I meant before she brought our food. What if my advice upset her? I've heard what waitresses will do to your food if you upset them.

I decided. "A hamburger, fries and coke," I blurted, looking up again. This time I had to look. I had to.

I avoided her eyes and stared at the offensive dangler. It was a nose ring and it had a chain that connected back to her ear. Cute! No! Ugly! But better than what I had thought.

As I waited for our meals to arrive, I was surprised at how her nose jewelry surprised me. After all, we used a lot of nose jewelry on the farm. Pigs got nose rings to encourage them to stop rooting. Cows who wanted to drink milk instead of make milk had anti-sucking barbs stuck through their nostrils. The bulls received a big brass ring with a chain tied to it. And, while it was surprisingly different, this young lady was wearing a nose ring and chain pretty similar to our bulls except we let the chain dangle.

Noses and nose jewelry were our major way of controlling livestock on the farm. Farmers know that where the nose points, the rest of the beast follows. We took advantage of that fact, but noses are different. The Creator has gifted each species with a remarkable, but different, nose. To compensate, we had different nose devices.

For pigs we had the snout handle. It looked like a large four-sided box wrench. Each end was a different size to accommodate different sized snouts. Simply slip one end over the snout or top of a pig's jaw and you had a nice come-along. Based on the vigorous squealing from the pigs I suspected the snout handle was quite uncomfortable. Of course, pig squealing is not always a good indicator of discomfort. Pigs are quite vocal whenever asked to do anything not related to food.

The big problem with the snout-handle (after getting it on the pig), was that if they resisted too vigorously you could easily break the snout, which then required extending an immediate invitation to breakfast at the big house.

For horses we had halters and bridles that pointed their noses in the direction we wanted their bodies to follow, but we also had a wicked little device called a nose knot. It was essentially a thumbscrew for the nose. It looked like a policeman's stubby nightstick. The cord the policemen put around his wrist was looped over the horse's nose. Twisting the nightstick then tightened the loop. You got some mighty strange looks from the horses as the loop tightened and their soft velvet nose took on the shape and tension of a water balloon.

This technique was used primarily as a distraction. While the horse was standing stiff-legged, staring down its nose wondering if you'd gone berserk, the vet would be sneaking up to the business end of the horse with a hypodermic the size of a carrot. The theory was that the horse's nervous system was not sophisticated enough to register pain at both ends of its anatomy simultaneously.

I believe we have successfully disproved that theory. When the hypodermic was punched into the backend of the horse, the expression of the front-end, and the resultant explosion, has proved to me that a horse's nervous system can process pain at both ends simultaneously.

Always, it was at that point that the horse tired of our shenanigans and promptly evicted us from its stall--nose knot and all.

The problem with the nose knot was that it was a one-time opportunity. No horse would allow you to put it on them a second time. Unfortunately, after the nose knot the same was true of a halter or bridle. It was a stupid way to wreck a good horse.

My big brother Duane, somewhere along the way, learned how to just give them shots. He loads up his hypodermic that has been used a hundred times and is as dull as a ten-penny nail. He stands right next to the thunder and lightening end of the horse and just gives the shot. (I'm usually standing back a bit so I don't get in his way.) They flinch a little, their eyes might get big, but it only hurts a second. Then they return to the treat of grain and molasses Duane had set out.

Not very exciting.

Now cows have a big rubbery nose that feels like wet plastic. For this model nose a nose pliers was invented. The jaws of the pliers end at spheres the size of marbles. The spheres never quite touch. This is to prevent mashing the inside of the nose. A rope was threaded through the ends of each handle of the pliers. Pulling on the rope closed the jaws which were inserted, one each, into the cow's cavernous nostrils.

Once the nose pliers were clamped on, a lot of the fight and disagreement left the cow. She would generally submit to anything: like the vet drawing blood from her neck, trimming the hair from her ears with a clipper or sawing off her horns with a bone saw. I was told that horns had the feeling and sensitivity of fingernails or hair, but cows didn't seem to like the sawing one bit.

Moving on to smaller noses, consider the chicken. No one has ever made a big deal about noses on chickens. In fact, chickens' noses have historically received less attention than hens' teeth. But to parody Shakespeare, "a 'nose' by any other name would smell just as sweet."

Abusing chickens was safer than working large livestock. It was less work once you learned how to avoid the beak and talons. Although, after mastering control of beak and talons I still took several severe wing-beatings on the head. Once the control aspect was mastered, I felt smarter than a chicken, and I confidently used the long-wire leg-catcher to snare hen after hen and deliver them to Mom and Dad who fitted each hen with aluminum spectacles. These opaque spectacles gave the hens a studious, intellectual appearance. The spectacles worked as blinders and prevented them from seeing. It wasn't that we wanted a coop full of blind chickens bumping around. We needed a cure for pecking. There had been an outbreak of pecking to the point that several hens had been killed and many more were bloodied.

The blinders effectively prevented the chickens who had acquired a taste for blood and cannibalism from seeing the bloodied head of their fellow chickens. Technically, chickens have eyes on the sides of their head; and they could see their bloodied companions, but when they pointed their noses at the victim, the victim disappeared behind the aluminum spectacles, and with chickens it truly is "outta sight. outta mind."

Well, my hamburger has arrived. I glance sideways at the waitress' nose ring. It doesn't shock me this time. In fact if you're going to have a nose ring, this one could be called tasteful, or interesting, or at least, different.

I look out the restaurant window. The summer afternoon heat draws butterflies to a mud puddle left from a morning thunderstorm. Thermals rise from the baking mud and the butterflies ride a breeze with the aimlessness only butterflies in the sun can have. It's nice to see a spot of "difference" in this city of concrete sameness.

The Crush
(Perspective)

The Crush
(Perspective)

Last night on the radio Garrison Keeler, the storyteller, made the point that as we grow older and put some time and distance between ourselves and our personal history, what happens is that the "hot" emotional stories we used to tell simply become "stories of life." Our judgment evaporates, and we become more tolerant. Events that once incited pain or emotion become simple history. Time grants us a perspective that allows us to talk about events in our lives that were once too "close," too "hot," or too emotive to report on without embroiling the reporting with our personal condemnation and judgment. The example he used was when a couple of his less desirable high school classmates (what we in Caledonia called "hoods"), packed up in an old Studebaker and went to live in California without jobs, and without addresses. Their actions certainly seem irresponsible from my "1960's attitude," but my "90's attitude" can view their migration West as an adventure; and of course with thirty years of successes and failures to report, it is easier to see the wisdom or folly of their actions. Now, thirty years later, Garrison was able to tell their story without getting involved.

This, I think, is one of the benefits of getting older. Age and time give you a different perspective on what happened in your life. Perspective is kind of like seeing your own nose from the side for the first time--same nose, different view. For example, my older siblings and I have always taken credit for teaching Mom and Dad how to be great parents. We feel that it was we older kids who got them used to the idea of parenting. We softened up the rules and helped both grow through those early years before parenting became second nature. I do believe that we did a darn good job. I think our younger siblings owe Alice, Duane and I a great deal of thanks for breaking in (and mellowing out) two of the greatest parents I could ever imagine.

I've been thinking about this "mellowing," this "gift of time" that gives you perspective, tolerance and insight into life. I know time has changed my opinion on what has happened and how I feel about it.

For example, the Iron Curtain has been dismantled and Communism and the Cold War is more of an embarrassing memory than a threat. Now, in a world without the Communists, I expect there to be peace and flowers everywhere in the world, and yet I do not remember a time when the world was as torn apart by wars as it is today. It seems there is a process of segmentation going on in the world that I do not understand and our language reinforces that segmentation. We have so many words that simultaneously describe:

- How someone is different than us;
- Why we can't get along with them;
- How we should act;
- The justification, philosophy, rational and morality of our actions.

For example, in South Africa it's Apartheid. One word describes it all. In the streets of America it's called racism; in government it's protectionism or nationalism or partisan; in religion it's called Hinduism, Judaism, Catholicism and dozens of other "ism's."

We have even invented new words like homophobia, "Ethnic Cleansing," DINKS (Double Income, No Kids), and gridlock to describe new forms of intolerance and separation.

A society is described by the words it uses; and, conversely, a society creates new words for what it considers important. I find it unsettling that we continue to define new forms of segmentation. These words point out how we are separate from each other and stand as irrefutable proof and justification that we can't get along with each other.

Well, I like to think that I am above such petty behavior.

Unfortunately, the world I see outside is only a reflection of my personal life. For example, when I think about my relationship with my ex-wife and how for the last years I have tried so very hard to be "separate" from her. It has been my only goal as far as she was concerned. I'm sure that my insistence on our separateness has not made her time any easier. Now I can rationalize and justify my actions, but I will spare you that rhetoric. Suffice it to say that while time has granted me perspective, and I judge all those nations and politicians and preachers who can't get along with their fellow man as fools; I find that I can't get along with the one woman who loved me, and gave me children, and lived with me as I gained perspective on life.

Should I have stayed with her? I really think that she deserved to be loved more than I was capable of. This way at least she has the chance to be loved, as she deserves to be, as do I.

But, am I happy with how things turned out? Well, when I was in high school, I had the world's biggest crush on Sally. It was a "crush" so big I never did anything except go deaf and dumb whenever she was near. She asked me once (probably the only conversation we ever had--well almost a conversation. She asked me a question and I immediately turned stupid.). She asked me, "If you could do your life over, would you do anything different?" I thought about that question for weeks and immediately reached the conclusion that my life had been executed perfectly. Not one action triggered regret, not one thought deserved rethinking. Well, so much for being an immortal, indestructible, all-knowing teenager. Today when I replay that question, I think I would do everything differently. Not because I did everything wrong, but because I know I can do things better and doing them the same would only be boring.

Am I happy with how things turned out? I like my life and I like myself. It has taken many years for me to get to this place despite all the support and love I've received from family. I have done some very hard and some very stupid things, and people have often wondered at my optimism and my consistently positive outlook. When they ask, I usually take credit for it by claiming to be strong or bright or lucky, but in truth I am loved. I have been blessed with a family that shares unequivocal, unquantifiable, unconditional love.

And this brings me back to the beginning. "Time" does grant you another perspective on life, but I don't think it includes any "understanding." I'm just as confused as ever. I don't understand why I have perfect health, joy, abundance, an understanding God, and a loving family. I don't understand. But, given the perspective granted by my years, it has spawned appreciation and gratitude for my good fortune and allowed me to give others greater latitude to do the things they must--no matter how strange their choices. Besides, I'm willing to wait another thirty years to see how things turn out for them. At the very least, it's guaranteed to be interesting.

Where Am I?
(I Don't Understand).

Where Am I?
(I Don't Understand)

I don't understand anything.

Now I think I'm smart, trainable and insightful, but when I look at life I have not been able to find anything I understand: common things, important things, nothing. I think! I feel! I know! I believe! But what do I understand? Nothing.

Gravity is an example of something we all think we understand because it is familiar, dependable and so experiential. Every time we drop a plate of food on our new carpet we demonstrate the predictability of the laws of gravity. Unfortunately, predictability is not "understanding." You may be able to predict that tiny, uncomfortable icehouses will populate our frozen lakes in Minnesota during the coldest part of the year, but you will never understand why? Even after hearing reasons from those who retreat into the icehouses, you wonder that there must be a reason even they don't understand.

Man's recourse, whenever he doesn't understand something, is to describe it and name it. Ever since Newton and his apple, scientists have been describing the features of gravity. Newton declared "The Law of Gravity" which deals with gravity's predictability, but does nothing to explain gravity. Scientists don't know how it works. They can't interrupt or recreate gravity so they content themselves with describing gravity and its effects.

There is nothing that surrounds us that we understand from "How do flowers grow?" to "How does your body convert a Snickers Bar into living tissue?" I mean, talk about an education system. If I asked you to teach a Snickers Bar, how to teach other Snickers Bars, to teach other Snickers Bars to turn a Snickers Bar into living tissue, you'd claim I'd had one too many Snickers. But that is what we do every time we munch on one of those tasty treats. I don't care if you are a doctor, scientist or nutritionist, no one understands "how" to turn air, water and rocks into living tissue. We can only take advantage of the process.

It would be comforting if we at least knew where we were. We like to respond with addresses and zip codes. Of course we know the names *we've given* the rivers and streets, but we are really a lost people set down on this blue marble hurtling through space. Since we don't know where we are, or where we are going, we have declared "here" home. Ever since the beginning we have regularly sent a brave soul to the top of a farther and farther ridge, and have received reports back that, relative to home, there is another ridge out beyond.

OK. OK. So maybe we don't understand what holds this world together (gravity), or any of the life forms on it, and maybe we are lost and it wouldn't hurt to ask for directions, but us guys understand mechanical things. Right? Alas, No. Mechanical things like car engines only have more parts that allow more extensive description and mask our lack of understanding. We may be able to predict the push or pull of parts and can describe how energy is stored, eliminated or controlled, but no one really understands combustion or electricity or nuclear power. It is a bit like Einstein discovering that energy can be reduced to

$E=MC^2$, but that discovery is like a child discovering $2+2=4$. Two plus two has always equaled four, just as $E=MC^2$ has always been true. The formulas simply allow us more extensive manipulation of the existing environment. It's a bit like building a table. At best, we can become good at manipulating the raw materials of this world because we don't create anything. We only rearrange pieces into different combinations and name those combinations "house," "cake," "car" or "computer". The theorem that "energy cannot be created or destroyed," reiterates that we are content to only change the shape of things provided; and, in the long run, are reassured that we can't wreck anything.

Another thing I don't understand is how the body remembers things. Take music for example. Being a musician, I know we store the music of scattered dots and staffs and flags and symbols that represent meter and tone and intensity in our bodies. And if we endure the tedium of repetition we can train our body to memorize the most intricate runs and the most difficult phrases. Once committed to memory it is like pressing a "Play" button on a tape recorder to recall the music. Only now, the music is alive. It is part of you. It comes from your heart; out your fingers; through your instrument, and into life. And like life, every playing is as different as a day, and each playing is filled with your soul, your thoughts, and your energy. Your body plays. It remembers which note when and which finger where. The body remembers the music. The mind interprets what the body remembers. And the body remembers forever.

Music itself is another mystery in our lives that is beyond understanding. Where does it come from? Where does it go when we stop playing? Maybe its infinite form is not meant to be compressed into understanding. Maybe it is only meant to be enjoyed and played with. Maybe it is like life as my Grandma Josey told me so many years ago. "Life," she said, "is like a bucket of water. You can splash and churn

the water all you want, and when you stop, the water returns to calm."
Maybe that's as close to understanding as we can get. Everything in this
world is provided for us to use and enjoy and care for. We can build
bombs or playgrounds. We can play music or march in cadence off to
war. We can manipulate the raw materials of this world into the most
marvelous shapes or the most deadly toxins, but understanding the stuff
itself is not our job. We need but decide and then suffer or enjoy the
consequences of our decisions.

Maybe it isn't necessary I understand this amazing world. Maybe
I can be content to turn on a light and use the electricity without
pondering the complexities of its generation and delivery, let alone its
creation. Perhaps it is enough that the earth knows how to turn sunlight
into flowers, and that a smile can melt the winter's snow, and that love
will heal a wounded heart. I don't need to understand how, but now
have the faith to know *it will*.

When Spring Arrives
(Beliefs)

When Spring Arrives
(Beliefs)

Tonight there is a new moon, a big moon the Indians call the "Beaver Moon" or the "Frogs Return Moon." Springtime is upon us, and I am filled with this feeling of joy and hope and anticipation that comes with all new beginnings. It recalls for me the many springtimes of my childhood, of working on the farm and the blessed arrival of the sun after the hard bitterness of our extended Minnesota winters. I remember those first brief warm days when the cats would stretch out and bask in the wind-sheltered sun on the south side of the silo. They would luxuriate there; their night eyes squinted shut against the brilliance until their coats became too hot to touch. I'd sit and pet and disturb their sunbath. They'd rub their face and back and tail against me and contribute far more energy to the petting then I did.

With my back pressed against the snow-white wall of the silo room, I was pleased by the warm grass; my eyes were closed against the brilliance, and I'd sit with a cat on my chest, its motor rumbling and cycling in time to my breathing and my stroking. Then the winter, still in the ground, would begin seeping through my trousers, chilling my bottom, and encouraging me to get on with spring, to get on with farming, and I'd leave the cats to their soak.

Spring was the time we'd open the garage, the corncrib, the machine shed or wherever we had stored the tractor and plow and disk, and roll or pull them into the sun, all shiny and greased and newly painted after a winter's overhaul. Then we'd head for the fields to turn the earth and discover what lay beneath its surface.

As a child, I'd walk behind the plow discovering grubs and gopher holes, angleworms and night crawlers. Dad would stop the tractor after a lap around the field to point out the straightness of his furl and answer my thousand questions about why some soil was brown and some black and hear my excitedness about the salamander the plow uncovered. It was a time of wonder and appreciation for the life that earth yields; a time of ignorance about the terror and trauma in the other parts of the world; a time of faith and trust in the two wise souls who agreed to be my parents and bequeath me the foundations for this marvelous vehicle called my body.

It was a time when I lived more in tune with the rhythm of nature. There was an urgency to spring. It was our opportunity to invest in a fall's harvest, and we needed to prepare the land for seed. "You plant corn when the oak leaf is the size of a squirrel's ear," my Dad advised.

"What size is a squirrel's ear?" I asked. "Do you use a baby squirrel or a big squirrel? Does it make a difference what color the squirrel is?"

Always asking a thousand questions I followed and learned. I took every chance to be underfoot until I became old enough to take my place on the tractor and provide some measure of real help. Then, of course, having done it; having driven the corn cultivator all day in the hot sun; having blistered my hands on the haying; having risen at dawn to do the milking; the magic of farming vanished despite the clear dawns and golden sunsets. Yes, despite the sweet fragrance of clover and the gentle droning of spring rain on tin roofs, despite the migrating return of the robin, the burst of flowers, the eclectic mating music of birds all day and frogs all night, despite the hum and husbandry of the honey bee and the birth of new calves--yes, despite being immersed in a world anew, of magic and life and potential beyond our reckoning-- at the ripe old age of fifteen I was jaded. This was old stuff, and I was bored beyond tolerance. I remember friends, town kids, visiting with wide-eyed amazement, and me not understanding their awe over the horses and cows and sheep, over woods to hunt, and buildings to explore and land to run and romp, over siblings always there to play, and over parents that cared. "Yea? That's us. So what's your point? Let's go to town to watch television."

Now I'm older but not really wiser. At best I stand a littler taller, but my gaze seems focused off in the distance, ignoring the miracles of life I step over.

When I think about life, I ponder about who I am and why I am, and I always get side-tracked by what I am: father, brother, son, computer guy--lots of titles that define different aspects of me. But all that I am reduces down to what I believe. My beliefs determine how I act, what I value, what my goals are and where I will go. It limits what I will do and not do, what I consider important, and what I consider trivial. It includes my concept of my God, my self, my purpose, and my peers who populate this greening earth. Our beliefs are our identity. Our beliefs make us who we are, how we are perceived and how we are accepted by others. Beliefs are the foundations of values and the ingredients of our principles. Our beliefs are the summation of our experiences and the interpretation of our purpose. Our beliefs encompass both the greatest and the most trivial parts of our lives. All my beliefs accumulate into the identity I call "me."

"Beliefs," I always believed, never changed. But now, to my surprise, my firm, unshakable, unchangeable concepts of who I am and what I believe changes every time I turn around.

As I get older, I start seeing patterns in life and a pattern I've noticed is that my beliefs seem to change significantly every seven years. Remember in the last chapter I noted how the body remembers? That the body can recall memories with a capacity and capability the mind cannot explain? In parallel, science tells us that every seven years we get a completely new body. Every cell in the body is replaced every seven years, and I've noticed that every seven years, I get a new set of beliefs. The arrival of each new body coincides with major periods in everyone's life. For example, when I was a child my beliefs about life, God, sex, parents and purpose were all different than now. I've noticed that for me, my basic beliefs changed with annoying regularity. Just about the time I think I have a handle on what is happening to me, all the rules change.

Ages 0 - 7; Childhood; Fantasy

Childhood is filled with spirits and ghosts, Santas delivering toys, and fairies trading treats for teeth. My niece, five-year-old Josey, came to me Easter morning, and with all the presence, gravity and sympathy a five-year-old can project, and after overnight contemplation of the story I had told, she said, "Uncle Larry, you didn't ride home on the bus with the Easter Bunny on Friday because the *real* Easter Bunny visited my house this morning and left my basket by the basement door." Think of a child's beliefs about the world, about parents, about themselves, and about God. A child sees no distinction between itself and the rest of the world. A child knows no right or wrong. The edges of you and yours and me and mine are blurred. A child is part of everything. Children walk and play with God and angels. We dismiss it as childhood. The sages insist it is innocence and wisdom and holds a set of beliefs to which we should aspire to return.

Ages 8 - 14; Youth; Adventure

The Catholic Church declares this period as "achieving the Age of Reason," and it is a time when you discover you were/are *wrong*. During this period the beliefs about God, parents, and self all change. God becomes a distant power rather than an equal or a playmate. Parents are idealized, and life is eternal and filled with unlimited potential. As a youth, I lived in trees and on rooftops. I built forts and weapons. I explored woods and rivers no man has seen before or since. It's a time of adventure. I realized that "*I*" am separate from "*you*," but believed everything was created for me.

Ages 15-21; Teenager; Puberty

This is probably the cycle of biggest changes in beliefs. Beliefs about parents, school, and God change again, completely. Parents fall from the pedestal of idealism to the pit of idiocy. You learn to block out religious inconsistencies that insult your intelligence or you become an agnostic. You believe that "you" are the center of a universe whose purpose is to serve and amuse you. God is in charge but not beyond manipulation as every apocalyptic crisis (from pimples to clothes to peer acceptance) is laid imploringly before God, always preceded with, "God, if you'll do this for me just once, I'll..." Then if these changes weren't enough, the very interesting subject of sexuality becomes more interesting and experiential.

Ages 22 - 28; Young Adult; Responsibility

Now in our twenties we have been raised and trained, and are expected to go out and amount to something. Parents and society are now expecting us to be productive and contributing members of society, and we are being prodded to "leave the nest." Now we notice that God hasn't answered any of our petitions--at least not as we requested and we begin to suspect that we are not the center of the universe. Generally, we feel we are being asked to stand on our own and in retaliation, we ask God to do the same. We believe we are separate from God and everyone, and in times of reflection wonder what happened? And who's in charge?

Ages 29 - 35; Adult; Career & Family

This is a time of "striving" and panicked, frantic energy to put together sense and purpose. Your priorities of children and family and community and career all seem to be number one. You notice on your list of important tasks and responsibilities that you didn't get put on your own list. You are not only separate from everyone else but feel like you are on the outside looking in. Then one day you pause with a breath clenched deep in your chest and you notice your parents have finally acquired some sense and wisdom. You exhale with a sigh that maybe there is some hope. Perhaps we can learn to understand and support each other. After all, all we have is each other. God, unfortunately, still seems to be busy somewhere else.

Ages 36 - 42; Mid-Life Crisis & Questioning

A time of change. There has got to be a better way. You're tired of the cynicism and materialism and competition. Your sense of self has dwindled into everybody else's rules and expectations. Your sense of purpose has been formed by somebody else's goals. You feel like a doormat and a meal ticket. Something has got to change. You may not know where you're going, but you're convinced you have to go. You figure it's about time that you had a talk with God and that you explain to Him how things should be.

Ages 43 - 49; Purpose and Focusing

It is hard to describe my beliefs now. I have always found it difficult to see myself. The past and future are clearer than the present. It's a bit of the "forest-for-the-trees" blindness. I can only say that now my life seems filled with lightness and joy. I think I'm in love with life, and in love. That alone may account for my blindness and make my judgment suspect. But I believe that life is good, that people have untapped and incredible potential, that life was meant to be filled with joy, that God is on our side, that He has not abandoned me, but that it was I who had abandoned Him.

Yes, life is good. Everything seems happier. My days are full, my nights more peaceful, my work more purposeful, and my play now pervades everything. And you know, since I believe this, it seems true. Not much has changed except my beliefs. True I've changed some circumstances, but my happiness doesn't come from where I work or live. More accurately, I believe work and home are happier because of my beliefs, rather than the reverse. My beliefs contribute far more to my happiness than my circumstances.

The world proves that beliefs determine circumstance. Beliefs are powerful. In October 1987, we (the American people) changed our minds about the value of stocks and the stock market crashed. It dropped 507 points and one-third of the wealth of America disappeared. But that's not so unique. Everything we value; in fact, the very concept of "value" depends upon our accepting a whole belief system. This happens in real estate all the time. The seller believes his land deserves one price, and the buyer believes a different price. Then everyone believes something different, and land prices drop from $1,000 an acre to $100 an acre, or jump to a new unreasonable high.

Also, I spent my entire life in the shadow of the Iron Curtain believing the Russians were our enemies. Now the Cold War is over, and they are our friends and allies. How did it happen? It was simply a change in beliefs.

Similarly, the whole world responds to our beliefs. Strong peoples hold strong beliefs and commit stupid, incomprehensible horrors that, given our beliefs, are simply crazy. Whether you look to Waco, Jonestown, Bosnia, the World Trade Center, or a dozen other parts of the world where man has lost his humanity, you may question the sanity of the rulers, but you cannot deny their commitment to their beliefs and the impact their beliefs have had on their part of the world.

I believe that since we have the power to make life worse, we also have the power to make it better. We are in charge. An advertising slogan for dieting is "Change your head, and the rest is easy."

Ages 50 - 56; ??? ???

As I reviewed my youth and my progress to here, I've noticed that I and others go through similar patterns in behavior. I've also concluded that we act and behave in certain ways because of our beliefs. But, I'm going to need some help with this and subsequent ages. Not having achieved this level I wonder if my parents have had similar shifts in their beliefs and in how they viewed the world? I'd like to sit and find out more about the amazing people I called "Mom and Dad" and perhaps learn something about them. Simultaneously, maybe I will be better prepared for the future if I know what to expect.

Don't judge the accuracy of these beliefs I've dispensed. Remember that this ranting is a "profunity" on how beliefs change and that at every age; no, at every instant, we cling completely to our current beliefs.

Are my beliefs correct? I don't think they are wrong, but I do suspect they are incomplete. And each time I rediscover a missing piece, all my beliefs are re-evaluated in the light of the new evidence. This openness has helped me accept others as they are. I may not understand, but now I know I don't need to. After all, each of us is different, and our individual experience of life is different from everyone else's. Some of us never lose that special appreciation of who we are, and where we are, and what life is meant to be; but for the rest of us, we need to spend our forty days (or is it forty years?) in the wilderness before we allow ourselves to again experience and appreciate life.

Now it is springtime. Our time of eternal potential. Spring is our time of optimism. No matter how hard the winters, spring will always return, someone must win the lottery, and there is the persistent story of the perfect, joyous relationship. Always the potential, spring is filled with marriages, births, and graduations. Spring is filled with life-punctuating events of hope-filled possibilities.

Spring is not for "doing over," but for going forward. If there was ever anything I would wish to "do over" in my life, it would be to have appreciated the youth I had, while I was having it. Since that option is not immediately forthcoming, I am content to appreciate the life I have now and those of you who have consented to share it with me.

A Surgeon's Bargain
(Communication)

The weather sure is wet these days. I know the extra moisture is causing a real calamity for the farmers, but I've always enjoyed the rain. I think it's because the arrival of rain interrupted our farm work. I remember pleasant rainy days spent puttering in the shop with the rain pattering on the tin roof as I built all sorts of wonderful things. The rains brought us cool comfort after a hot, sweaty afternoon of haying. The rains cleared the air, washed the cows, filled the pond, and freed me from the endless miles of corn cultivating.

Thunderstorms were always my favorite weather as they broke around us on our protected home on the top of the bluff. The storms didn't break over us. They broke around us. Maybe it was foolishness on my part, but in the certainty of God's protection and care for us, I never feared the storms. Late at night when the crash and flash of nature would explode around the house, I'd wake and stand at my upstairs bedroom window and watch the yard turn from India-ink black to noon-time brightness, and then I'd count--one thousand one, one thousand two, one...**CRACK! Rumble**, Rumble, rumble. And I'd stand there at my window covered with goose bumps from the storm's chill and from anticipation, staring owl-eyed into the darkness, eyes dry straining to see something, anything. Then flash, flash, flash and the lightning fills the yard. The tractor doors on the corncrib flap in the wind and a broken branch is rolled across the yard in the freeze-frame steps of lightning flashes. The stop-action lightning freezes the pelting, wind-driven raindrops into polished, frozen-firm, glass beads. The lightning-captured image imprinted on my retina gradually fades as the lightning plunges me back into darkness and the following thunder thumps my chest and shakes the house.

I yawned and wondered if it was "raining pitchforks and hammer handles," or "raining cats and dogs." This I decided was "hammer handles." I crawled back into bed with the Sky Titans still clashing and absently noticed my bedroom wall animated by lightning-cast shadows of wind-whipped branches. Then, without a concern, I went to sleep knowing my safety was assured in the heart of the storm.

The certainty I held then as a young lad is with me where I stand today; completely protected, my safety assured, in a world where whole countries are being torn apart by the loss of their humanity. But we are part of the world, and when I look at the problems of the world and any problems that are dogging me personally; when I stop to think of why and what causes the world's problems and my problems, they are almost always "communication failures." Communication failures because someone doesn't understand, because someone didn't take the time to explain, or because someone didn't take the time to listen. Communication isn't always easy.

I spent the holiday with Mary Kris' family, and I noticed a communication difference between her family and my family. It's not better or worse, just a difference in the style of "group talk." In my family *"The Speaker Yields."* In Mary Kris' family, *"The Speaker Continues."* Let me explain what this means.

The Speaker Yields: When my siblings do "group talk" there is the group conversation. This means only one person talks at a time, but that person can be interrupted at any time, by anyone, and take the conversation in any direction. Usually, nobody gets to finish anything. The result is that after an entire weekend of listening to this style of "group talk," I can go home and feel that I didn't talk to anyone, and that I don't know what anyone is doing.

The Speaker Continues: When Mary Kris' family does group talk, you cannot interrupt another person's story. Speakers are allowed to tell their story completely. You are generally not encouraged to add reinforcing comments or supporting facts. Side comments are ignored and the monologue continues until complete. If there is something that must be said, a second or third simultaneous conversation is started, and I'm dizzied trying to keep track of both commentaries. Usually, I lose track of both or confuse the two.

The difference is in style. Every family or group has its style of communicating that works. One style is not necessarily better. Tony Robbins says that the success of communication "is the result you get." If it works, it's good.

There are few things that can tie a family together as closely and as tightly as communication. Many times, no, every time, when two people try to live together or work together, the quality of that relationship is determined by their ability to communicate with each other. Their communications express their appreciation of each other, help set joint goals and priorities, and help coordinate the energies to achieve those goals. There are a lot of requirements for successful communications, but first you need communication skills.

When I think about what skills have served me best, I go back to the hours Mom spent teaching me to say my own name. The "L" sound was tough for me. It didn't flip off my teeth like it was supposed to. Instead it dribbled down my chin and "Larry" was a tongue-twisting "Ware-Wee." I was offered the prize of going to school, to first grade, if I could learn to pronounce my own name. I felt very smart and capable from Mom's attention and praise and although there were times of frustration and inevitable boredom in school, school was my prize. There was nowhere I preferred to be. Even today I get excited just being on a college campus. When I step on campus, I feel something quite pleasurable--an accomplishment?, a level of performance?, prestige?, smart? I feel good! There is so much to learn in this life. There is little else I enjoy more. For me, the beginning of that love of learning and knowing the reward of achievement was first instilled in me during the hours spent trying to teach my uncooperative tongue to say its own name.

But more than verbal ability is required to communicate. You also have to listen.

When I was eleven I went into the hospital for minor hernia surgery on my right side. Lugging 20-gallon milk cans caused the hernia. No one had to tell me what was going to happen during the surgery. I *knew* what to expect. Three years earlier, when I was just a little kid, I had my left side repaired in a similar operation. Nothing to it. Especially since this time the doctor promised not to make me inhale ether which turned the light behind my eyes to a broken-egg-yellow and made me sick. I now appreciate it when my big brother Duane asks a hospitalized friend, "Were you sick when you came here? Or did they make you sick?"

I remember refusing to breathe the volatile ether. The smell was horrid. I fought and squirmed under the operating table straps, but I was cinched to that table like a saddle to a horse. I whipped my head left to right and the nurse tracked my head movements and waited for me to breathe. My chest began to burn, and I couldn't get away. I pleaded with her to wait just a second so I could take another breath, but the pleading cost me more breath. Finally I risked taking only the shallowest breath, and then the yellow darkness swept away my consciousness.

This time I was promised "no ether."

This time the nurse made jokes and flipped the flipper attached to a needle in my arm as I counted backwards. "100, 99, What do I do when I get to zero? 98,..." and I went to sleep expecting to wake up to toys, all the ice cream I could eat, and all the attention I could stand. Instead there was a buzzing in my head as consciousness crept to the edge of my recovery room bed and shouted that something was wrong, terribly wrong. I had bandages in the wrong place--close, but definitely in the wrong place, and I hurt.

It turned out that in addition to doing a fine job of repairing my hernia, the doctor also gave me a first-class appendectomy. And, since he was in the neighborhood and there was no other patients waiting, he threw in a circumcision. At that first, fuzzy, semiconscious moment, I didn't know or care about the appendectomy, but I almost busted a stitch trying to sit up to see what the circumcision had done to me. But then consciousness abandoned me and my panicked, clumsy exploration had to wait.

Later when I was fully conscious, Mom tried to explain the circumcision and talked about hygiene as I laid there holding my bandages, feeling betrayed, repeating, "But why?"

And yet, I had been told. When I am honest with myself, I was told. But I "knew" what to expect--toys, attention and ice cream in that order. Long medical terms like appendectomy and circumcision didn't mean anything to me. It was classic communication shutdown. Since I knew what to expect, and what I wanted, I stopped listening, and then was angered because I was the only one surprised.

It was sometime after healing and growing up that I promised myself that I would explain everything to my kids, including sex. Still later, after I had kids, I found out that it's not so easy to talk to them. Communication never is.

My plan was to talk to my kids early and often so that sex and body parts were natural and easy. Their first response was, "Why are you telling me this?" They actually would have been more interested in discussing rock formations on the backside of the moon. Since I started early, the information was also about as useful.

Later their "Cut-Dad-Off-Quick!" response was "I know all about it." My daughter, now nineteen, told me one of her classmates was pregnant and seeing the thoughtful look on my face immediately added, "That doesn't mean you have to give me a lecture on birth control." Her comment and the transparency of my thoughts surprised me because my mind had already formed the rough outline of a "lecture," and I was looking for a "catchy" opening that would make my advice more palatable.

No matter how "catchy," communication requires that both parties participate or your communication becomes a one-sided lecture or sermon. Trying to communicate with my kids has revealed to me that communication has to be a joint effort so that the product of communication (understanding) is achieved.

For communication you need someone willing to give information, someone willing to accept it, and we need to realize that everyone communicates differently (style). But we also need something else-- existing knowledge. Both parties to the communication have to already know and believe what is being communicated. For example, my older brother Duane was the scoundrel who told me all about sex. What he said was preposterous. He had to be lying.

"How come I never heard about this before?" I demanded. "And you take back what you said. I'm going to tell Mom what you said." But I could never tell anyone what my big brother claimed Mom and Dad had to accomplish to have children.

I never believed a word of it.

In that case communication failed because although I listened, I was being told something I didn't already know. It didn't fit my paradigm. This is very common in the world. People will not believe something new. New concepts or ideas are discounted and ignored if people don't already believe 95% of what you're communicating. Tall Tales or Liars Clubs, fiction and storytellers of all kinds are successful if they are able to weave what you already know and believe is true with the tiniest bit of the preposterous.

A politician gets elected not because he has new ideas, but because he has the same ideas as his electorate. All the posturing and stumping politicians do, is to convince you they don't have any new (scary) ideas, and that *they think like you.* The politician who expresses the will of the majority wins. The obvious contradiction in communication is that in order to communicate you need to avoid anything your audience doesn't already understand and believe.

The words we use can make us think we are getting something we're not. Is it a cliché or is it a sound bite? Is it a hearing aid or is it an assistive listening device? Did the politician lie or did he answer cautiously? Is someone short or vertically challenged? Is it genocide or is it ethnic cleansing? I think it's just marketing--wrapping the same-old-stuff in new clothes. It also points out how the tools of communication can be effectively used to foster misunderstanding.

Well, I think I'm getting "profune" again. What I am trying to say is that because all this "stuff" gets in the way, the only way we can communicate with each other is with great helpings of patience and love and gentleness and by repeating ourselves. Every time we say something, only a fraction is understood. So we need to keep trying. If someone doesn't understand, try again and again and again. Between each try it is best if we check to see if greater understanding is reached. The cycle of communication should be: try, check, try, check, try, check, etc. It is probably best if you try something different each time. Don't repeat yourself. If it didn't work the first time, why play it again?

I believe we all want the same things: to be loved, valued, and able to contribute to life. When I remember this, it makes it easier to understand others. Every communication is an attempt to establish that love, value and contribution. It's just that when someone is angry or scared or holding up a liquor store, it's hard to believe they want to "contribute to life." Their actions demonstrate that they may not feel loved or valued.

My parents taught me very young that I was loved and valued and praised my every contribution. It was this constant communication from them to each of us that gave me the security to sleep through raging storms, that instilled in me this unshakable confidence that we are more than we appear, that we have talent and capacity still untapped, and that we must really *be something* to have received a parent's love.

Wild Pig Hunt
(There's Always Hope)

Screams. Pain. Nightmare sounds of terror and torture. They were loud, long, fearful pleading sounds starting with lungs full and continuing to lungs forced empty. The repeating bursts of tortured agony drew me to its source. I moved from sunlight into darkness with stiff wooden movements, wanting to run, unable to stay away, drawn like a moth to a light. Compelled, I moved into the darkness toward the screams. In the silence between the squeals pleading for release I could hear the shouts of men. My groping hands found the top of a solid board pen made of wood, made of old, unpainted boards covered with years of dried accumulations of farm stuff. My eyes adjusted to the darkness. I pulled myself up on my toes to peer into the pen and watched in wide-eyed, scared-dumb silence as my Dad, my older brother and a hired man worked with the squealing, screaming pigs.

My Dad had rented the McKey's land with this old hog house for the season. There on that old, empty, falling-down farm, he was raising pigs. It was an interesting, exciting place for a young boy to visit. Having been unused for so long, the barns and outbuildings were surrounded with full-grown elephant ear, burdock, and bull thistles. There were forests of weeds towering seven feet tall that were amenable to sheltering small kids and having secret trails carved through their denseness. Trails that became tunnels. Tunnels that became magic pathways to other worlds that only a child can enter.

Then there was the barn. It was small but with a cavernous hayloft. A "years-ago" painted red barn; painted warm to capture the sun with a paint that didn't chip or peel, but turned to dust under decades of pressure from the wind and sun. Only a few windows still held panes of old, dusty, wavy glass with spider webs in their corners. Most were broken or empty. Now sky and clouds and pigeons moved in and out of the holes in the roof. The moss-covered, split-cedar shingles along the roof's edge gave the roof a green tinge. It was a barn with character and history--family history where a couple cows with names and personalities supplied the family with milk and butter.

The abandoned white board house stood on the high ground at the end of a long dirt driveway. The house was an icon of mystery, and I was a young boy of five with an afternoon of exploring to accomplish. I had been at the house earlier only stopping to press my forehead against a dusty, uncurtained window on the open porch. I framed my eyes with my hands and stared at the abandoned fragments of a family's history: an old straight-backed chair, a picture calendar on the wall, some yellowed newspaper on the curled, cracked linoleum, faded wallpaper with flowers and large wounds of plaster showing, the rounded end of a bathtub peeking through a far door, and the large trapdoor in the living room floor leading--where? I imagined the adventure that lay under that trapdoor. I imagined it leading down stairs to hidden passages, underground rivers, dungeons, secret societies, or treasure secured against attack from Indians or pirates or vampires. My young mind was keen for danger and adventure. My window surveillance complete, I opened the spring-loaded screen door and hopefully tried the inside door. It was locked. I turned and ran off the porch, the screen door slamming behind me, and headed round back to the rope swing.

The rope swing was an old, long, two-inch thick rope. To ride this one-rope swing, you sat on the overhand knot tied into its end. It wasn't very comfortable and didn't lend itself to "pumping" like regular "seat swings." To get it going you ran past the rope while holding onto it until the upswing lifted you off the ground. Then you wrapped your legs around the rope and slid down to the knot, keeping your legs clamped together. Being a one-rope swing it would spin around, out of control, and I would lean back to slow my spin and watch the tree turn around me in the sky above me.

If I was foresighted, I would fly onto the rope with a pocketful of grapes and eat until my mouth became tender and contemplate my young life while staring into the canopy of leaves framed in blue sky.

On this long ago summer day, left to myself, I explored and revisited all my secret places. Now I was safe under a canopy of grapes scratching the damp, cool ground with my fingers. The sunlight filtered through the grape leaves filling my hiding place with golden-green, ambient light. The veined leaves that protected and sheltered the young grapes from direct sun could not, however, keep out the noise of the squealing pigs. I had been told to stay out of the hog house. I was too small to help with the pigs, but I knew what was happening.

A pig's favorite food is the tender roots hidden just beneath the ground, and their flat noses are designed perfectly for rooting--for turning the grass upside down. Pigs use their snouts like plows to expose tender, tasty roots. They make a mess by eating everything, roots and all. In their wake they leave raw, open ground. That is great if you want a mud hole, or if you are Mother Nature and you want to plant new seeds, but farmers want to decide what, where, and when to plant. You don't want a pig plowing the ground and eating the sod. A bigger problem for farmers was that once a pig put its head down, it would follow its nose right under the fence. Three-foot high hog-wire is effective for keeping pigs in their place unless the pigs can get a nose-hold under the bottom of the fence. Then they can lift up the fence and walk under as easily as a kid crawling under a blanket. Dad was regularly finding his pigs in the field next door and decided it was time to stop the rooting.

To keep the pigs from rooting, Dad was putting "rooting rings" in their noses. In theory, inserting the nose rings wouldn't hurt. It was a simple operation much like having your ears pierced. The nose ring did not prohibit rooting, but rather made rooting uncomfortable, and with other sources of food available, rooting just wasn't fun.

The problem with pigs is that you can't easily explain that something won't hurt (much). Also, Dad raised these pigs on a deserted farm, and they were not used to being handled. There wasn't a pig in the bunch who wanted a nose ring, and that meant Dad and Duane had to argue with the pigs and force each one to hold still while they inserted the nose ring.

Each pig squealed louder than the one before it and that scared the following pig until the whole herd was frightened. I listened to the screams until I couldn't stand it any more. I had been sent away a couple times, but once more I headed for the sounds. This time I would make myself small. No one would see me. I crept toward the tortured sounds, and down the aisle between the pens. The squealing stopped. Voices. "Only a couple left. Grab that one." More squealing. "Don't let it get away!" I pressed my body against the outside of the pen, stretched up on my toes to see over the wall to peek into the pen, and came face-to-face with a fear-crazed pig. It slobbered drool on my hand as it stood on its hind legs with its front ankles hooked over the wall of the pen. Inches away, it didn't see me. It was looking over my head at the out-of-doors--at freedom. I jerked myself backward to the far side of the aisle as the pig jumped or crawled over the wall. Grunting and crying, it trotted to the half-door at the end of the hog house, scrambled up and over the half-door, and disappeared.

Then a second and third pig were in the aisle with me. My Dad yelled, "Stop them!" The two pigs brushed past, ignoring me. Following the lead of the first escapee, they stood on their hind legs at the half door, front ankles hooked over the top, hind feet clawing up the door propelling them to freedom. I stood there stunned. "Stop them! Go after them!" my Dad shouted, and he and my brother Duane were now out of the pen. I was shaken out of my frozen stupor and sent to head them off and to chase them back to the barn, but it was not to be.

Those three pigs had gone crazy. They became wild. Any veneer of domesticity was gone. Fear and survival drove them. The sight of man was now enough to propel them over or through fences. I realized then that fences are really only guidelines for farm animals. There isn't a fence around that can keep in an animal who really wants out, and the dilapidated fences around this aged, rented acreage fell before the terrorized exit of those three crazed pigs.

Well, we tried. We chased and followed until we were exhausted. Then we returned to take care of the rest of the pigs who had forgotten all about the screaming and squealing and were happily getting used to their new nose jewelry.

My Dad and brother spent the next week trying to catch up with the three escapees. Their efforts gradually increased: first on foot, then using the jeep, then on horseback. Each attempt failed. The pigs had scattered. They weren't running in a nice tidy flock. The only consistency was that all three had gone crazy. Whenever they would catch sight of man, they would turn tail and run at full speed, straight through anything. Reports started coming back to my dad about raided corncribs, ravaged gardens, or a lone pig sighting.

The reports of damage increased. Every raided granary in the county was blamed on the three pigs, so my Dad organized the only wild pig hunt ever held in Houston County. I think the hunt was organized based partly on his deer-hunting techniques, which I would learn when I became older, and based partly on the newsreels shown in the Caledonia movie theater that showed African natives spread out in a line, driving wild boars or gazelles or elephants toward the great white hunter.

That was how we started out. Dozens of friends and neighbors showed up. A neighbor kid arrived with a .22 caliber rifle loaded with birdshot and my Dad laughed at him and said, "You can't kill a pig with birdshot. You'll just make them crazy."

The kid said, "You already drove them crazy. The birdshot might at least make them turn if they charge."

The hunt started. Men armed with deer rifles were stationed ahead of the drivers who fanned out in a long thin line. Some were on foot. Others were on horseback. I was in the jeep with Mom and I begged her to follow them until they came to a fence line we couldn't cross. Then we went home where Mom prepared the traditional on-the-job thrashing crew lunch of Kool-aid and bologna sandwiches.

It took several drives, but the hunt was successful. Sadly, one pig was shot and the meat was wasted because the pig had been run so hard before being shot. Someone asked, "Why can you eat deer after a deer has been running, but you can't eat pig?" Beyond declaring that this was different because one was pork and one was venison, no one knew, and the meat was not saved. The second pig was unceremoniously taken, but the third pig escaped. There was much discussion afterwards about this smartest or craziest pig. Theories were presented how best to hunt this last one. Detailed stories were told and retold of a glimpse or suspected glimpse of this last pig. Its strength and speed was increasing with each retelling. It now ran through barbed wire fences like they were spider webs. It easily outran men and horses. Board gates were climbed easily as stairs, and logs were useful camouflage. This last crazed, wily pig held no fear of man, was intent on keeping its freedom, and avoided every hunt with uncanny simplicity.

Then, everyone left.

Since this last pig could avoid large groups of hunters, my dad decided on a solitary hunt--a stakeout. There were numerous reports of pig tracks near ponds, but it's difficult to tell the difference between deer tracks and pig tracks. So it took some observation and wild woods tracking on Dad's part to determine which pond this last pig was visiting. He finally decided on a small pond a mile from the house. For nights he would rise in the middle of the night to go sit in the woods overlooking the pond. Finally, just before dawn, when he was cold and tired from sitting up all night and working all day, he heard the quiet grunting and snuffling of a pig--a cautious pig. It stopped at the edge of the grass and looked across the pond to make sure all was clear. Then cautiously it stepped out of the shadows into the pre-dawn moonlight to get a drink. Dad raised his rifle as the pig stepped up to the edge of the pond. The pig paused, looked into the shadows and put its head down to drink. Dad took careful aim and squeezed off one shot. The pig screamed and dove into the pond. Mortally wounded, but not dead, the pig thrashed the waters, and my Dad ran to the pond's edge, set down his rifle and waded into the water with his knife to finish the job and to keep the pig from sinking to the bottom of the pond. Finished, he dragged his family's food up onto the bank.

Thus ended the only wild pig hunt ever held in the county.

Yet, despite my knowledge of the fate of the three pigs, whenever I walk the woods and come across a patch of ground that has been freshly plowed by the soft shovel-nose of a pig, I remember when the three made it to freedom, and I imagine that there is one who still survives, free of fences and nose rings.

The Jaws of My Jeans
(The Miracle)

The Jaws of My Jeans
(The Miracle)

Fall is here and school has started. I left late for work and got caught behind a school bus and watched worried parents escort their tiny children onto the big orange school bus.

My big sister Alice was charged with delivering me to first grade on my first day at Catholic Central Grade School. Years later, I found I had skipped kindergarten. Some say it was because kindergarten hadn't been invented yet. I believe it was because I was so smart I was automatically promoted.

It was my first day of school and Alice's fifth year. To put me at ease Alice told me the nuns would beat me if I misbehaved. She told me the nuns had ropes tied around their waists that they used to whip especially naughty children. If the nuns had killed any children, the nuns could tie a hangman's knot in their whipping rope. This nun had three knots in the rope that belted her habit. I found out later that the three knots symbolized the good Franciscan's vows of poverty, obedience and chastity (or ain't got none, don't want none, never had none). But I didn't know that when Alice deposited me in the first grade classroom.

When the door closed, I and 35 other panicked, misinformed five-year-olds were left alone with our worst nightmare. The only time I screamed more in first grade was when I caught myself in my zipper and couldn't get it unstuck. The good Franciscan came into the boys' lavatory and released me from the jaws of my jeans. After that I could see there was a gentler side to the Sisters of St. Francis.

Another part of the sister's habit was a huge rosary. It had beads the size of marbles and a crucifix as big as the one hanging from the good sister's neck. She kept the rosary looped over her waist rope, and it hung next to the hangman vow knots, ready to be fingered if there was a spontaneous outbreak of rosary. Frequently, as we waited quietly for the morning mass to begin, kneeling with only our eyes peering over the pew in front of us, I would hear the beads tap-tap-tapping on the back of the pew behind us.

Prayers were always a first and last resource for our family. Being Catholic it seemed only prayers on your knees counted. Aside from the daily mass before school, the noon visitation, the prayers at the start of each class, at lunch and at the end of day, there was the family rosary before bed. The rosary is a wonderful, rhythmic, mantra-like ritual that Catholics use when they want to do the most, and when they don't know what else to do. It is used to provide a meditative posture (on the knees, of course) and the droning repetition occupies the body and mind so the spirit can get something accomplished.

With the arrival of the eighth child, I think Mom decided we needed to get big things accomplished. So every night the lights would dim. The TV went off. Homework was put down and we each took turns leading the rosary through the Glorious Mysteries, the Sorrowful Mysteries and the Guiltful Mysteries that related the major events of Christianity.

Having a rosary was not a requirement to saying a rosary, but we needed bigger accomplishments so Mom procured a bigger rosary. It had beads the size of lima beans. As we knelt around the dim living room in the holy light of a single votive candle, the leader of the rosary thumbed and fingered his or her way along the huge beads. Since the leader-rosary was the size of five pocket rosaries, I felt we accomplished five times the praying. When I suggested we only needed to pray one-fifth as often, Mom worried about the value of the math I was supposed to be learning from the nuns.

Mom's solution to every problem started with prayer. The electric bill needed to be paid--we were on our knees. School was starting and eight kids needed shoes and shirts--an extra rosary or two. A neighbor is sick, their cow dies, or their barn burns--prayers until your knees are permanently creased.

The problem with prayer is that it often appears to be a one-way conversation. It would be nice to know that someone is listening. Yes, I know what Mom always taught about the presence of God, that He is omnipresent, always and everywhere. Despite that, I occasionally need some proof--a test.

Years later and living in the city, as a test, I once made hundreds of cars and their drivers disappear. It was a traffic jam that evaporated.

It was a miracle.

Rush hour in Minneapolis is seldom fun or fast. Like most big cities there are too many cars all jockeying for the same space of freeway. There are predictable bottlenecks that guarantee long lines of traffic creeping forward at stop-and-go or slow-and-go speeds.

It was winter. I was traveling from one side of the city to the other. The roads were all backed up. I tried a couple impatient, male-type end-runs (shortcuts) around the traffic and lost ground. I was grumpy and frustrated, so I started to pray. My prayer went something like, "Hey! Why is traffic like this?"

"THAT IS THE WAY TRAFFIC IS," came the patient response.

"Yea, well that's stupid. If you're really God and you are really here, get rid of this jam."

"OK."

Almost immediately the traffic congestion disappeared, and I began moving. I was surprised but not convinced. After all, it could have been a coincidence.

I needed a bigger test.

I was coming to the Interstate I-694 Mississippi River crossing. That bridge was backed up on good days, and today even the good roads were clogged from one of the winter's first snowfalls.

This bridge was on my way to work. I crossed it twice a day, every day, for years. I described the bridge to my kids as "Minnesota's Greatest Tourist Attraction" because people drove for miles and waited in long lines just to have the experience of driving across this very special bridge. I also described it as a "graven image" and we, its faithful servants, came twice daily to wait in line to worship in a ritualistic crossing. Then I told them the story of the "Three Billy Goats Gruff" and the ugly troll who lived under the bridge. That was why we always crept across the bridge so slowly (to keep from waking the troll and being eaten).

You have to understand, I've spent hours, nay, I've spent days, waiting in line to cross this bridge.

The bridge would be an impossible test.

"Hey!" I said in my prayerful voice. "That was just a piddly little traffic jam. If you're really here, fix the traffic at the bridge."

"OK."

It happened. I sailed right across the bridge with my mouth open and without anyone in front of me. I mean it was wide open (the bridge and my mouth). I was impressed. It was a miracle.

I have been told that "there is no order of difficulty to miracles."[1] Miracles just are. One is not more difficult or more grand than another. I drove across the bridge wondering if the hundreds of cars I had expected there had been vaporized, or delayed? In any case, I hoped they were not angry with where they were just so that I could have my miracle.

I was very pleased with my miracle. It was nice to know that God is around, and that He does occasionally get involved.

The next time I came across the bridge the same thing happened. No traffic jam. And the next time. And the next. What happened to the traffic? This bridge was unchanged, untouched except for the miracle. There had been no repair work done on the bridge before, during, or after the miracle. I knew, because I crossed that bridge, very slowly, twice a day. Amazing! Then it was explained to me. There was no miracle. A new bridge had been built and opened a couple miles upriver. The traffic had been diverted to the new bridge. It was just that simple. Hmmh!

No miracle.

Then I remembered a story about a little girl who wanted desperately to believe in God[2]. She went out onto a balcony on a summer night, closed her eyes and said that if she saw a shooting star when she opened her eyes, then she would know that God existed--then she could believe.

---

[1] A Course in Miracles

[2] The Journey Without Distance, by Helen Schulman

When she opened her eyes, the sky was filled with shooting stars. She was very happy. She believed God had answered her. She had experienced a miracle.

The next day she was told to look for shooting stars since this was the time of year for them. The little girl was crushed. The shooting stars she saw were expected. They would have happened anyway. She lost faith in her miracle with the angry statement that "If that was a miracle, God, You could at least make me believe in it."

Me? I'm back at my miracle bridge saying, "Yeah God. If you went through all that trouble at the bridge, you could at least make me believe in it!"

"OK."

(I've got to learn to keep my mouth shut.) As it is with all challenges, prayers, or petitions, none ever go unanswered. When you refuse to listen to the small patient Voice, you get reinforcement. A friend came to me and gently told me that "Miracles are natural." This reminded me of the healings I had experienced: the cold that had run its course, the cut that finally went away, the broken bone that stopped hurting. In every case the healing wasn't a wonderful, mystical experience. It was something very natural. It was so natural, in fact, that I almost always did not notice the healing. At some point I would recall that I had been "hurt" and try to figure out which hand. Sure enough, I would search and discover a scar, a memory, a reminder of the pain, but nowhere could I find a declaration of when the healing occurred. It was always that natural. It was not ecstasy. It was not pain. It was natural.

My miracle at the bridge continued. For the rest of the winter and all summer long I sailed across my bridge. I got quite used to the smooth flow of traffic, but I couldn't cross the bridge without remembering. I wondered which is the greater miracle: to have hundreds of cars vaporized so that I could cross the bridge alone, or to have life arranged so that not only I, but also the other hundreds of travelers, can cross the river without causing each other pain?

I now have a new definition of a miracle. It is a natural event, a healing. When things go well, when things go like they are suppose to, when there is no pain, when everything feels right--that is the time of miracles.

Despite my initial skepticism, I became convinced that something did happen. I wondered how long the miracle would last? If there were an accident or a jam on the bridge, would that be the end of the miracle?

I wondered.

A year went by. I was working between the Minnesota River and the Mississippi River. The people going five miles south must cross the Minnesota River. The people going ten miles north must cross the Mississippi. River crossings are always more difficult in bad weather. In December a blizzard was working its way across the city, and I knew the roads would be clogged. A ten-minute trip could easily take an hour. As I got on the freeway headed north, the southbound traffic was already backed up the full five miles to the Minnesota River Bridge. I drove north past another solid mile of stopped, southbound traffic, and I thought of my bridge. How would my miracle handle this rush hour blizzard?

Would the miracle end?

I wanted the miracle to continue. Aside from it being "my" miracle, I enjoyed the fast ride across the bridge. I drove north, trying to rationalize how the miracle could continue in spite of a jam at the bridge. These were exceptional circumstances. I could barely see the road. Traffic was creeping. I rationalized that if the bridge were jammed today and flowing tomorrow, it would be OK. I continued north and as I came to a major freeway intersection, I was saying to myself, "Well Miracle, if you are going to continue, you are going to have to do something extraordinary."

"**OK**."

And eight snow plows pulled out onto the freeway ahead of me, and began a curb-to-curb cleaning of the freeway. It was like a scene from the movie "Airport," and I was the lead car. These eight snow-plowing-sanding-dump-trucks cleared the four-lane freeway the next five miles. They got off the freeway just in front of my bridge, leaving no one in front of me except an aging Cadillac waiting its turn at the freeway access meters that controlled access to the bridge. The old Cadillac pulled out onto the bridge as I entered the ramp and I slowed to about 40 miles per hour as the timing light turned green for me. There I was--sailing across the bridge without a problem--during rush hour--during a blizzard.

There is no order of difficulty to miracles.

The nice thing is that our prayers are answered, no matter how we phrase them. I remember this as a caution, because every thought, every desire, can come back as an answered prayer. Our problem is that we are, everyday, moving forward into an unknown future. Every day is our first day there, and we don't know what to pray for. But, just like that scared, misinformed first grader, the suspected terrors of this life are often more imaginary than real. And like that first grader, I've found that if I pay more attention to life, I find that every situation is part of my own doing. For example, if I pay attention, I won't have to be rescued from my own clothing. My comfort is that some sweet angel will be there to help even when it's my stupidly that brings them there.

As a farm family, I believe that we lived a charmed life. Whether I was scampering across the barn rooftop or doing a high-wire walk across the big haymow door, whether we children were operating heavy machinery or wandering the woods, we were never unsupervised or unguarded. Our prayers went before us, our angels went with us, and our faith in things unseen was reinforced by daily miracles of simple safety and health. I just have to be reminded occasionally.

"OK."

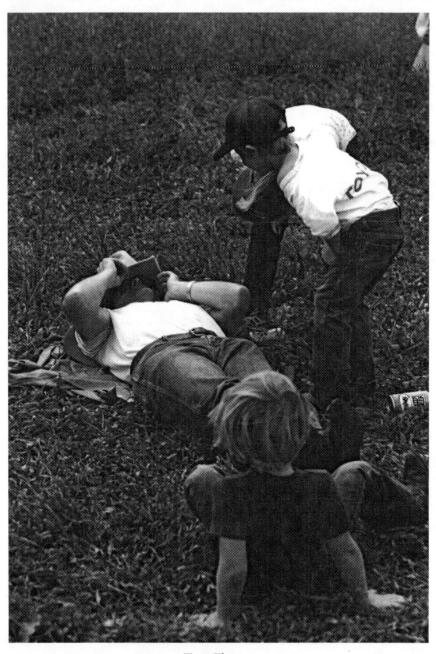

Time Thieves
(What to do with Time???)

Time Thieves
(What to do with Time)

"I saved 3½ seconds."

"What?"

"I found how a computer can save 3½ seconds on one transaction," I said in response to Mary Kris', routine question about how my day was. "It took all day, but I did it."

"You spent eight hours to save 3½ seconds?"

"Nine hours actually, but it was worth it. Those 3½ seconds will be saved billions of times." I saved 3½ seconds. It's my job. I'm a computer guy. Time is scarce so we look everywhere for ways to save time. It's the efficiency of business today. Everything is packed together. Life is hectic. We all want to save time, but I keep wondering what is happening to all the time my computer is saving me. The more time I save at my computer, the less time I have. I now have on-line banking. The computer balances my checkbook, pays my bills, and transfers funds. I never have to go to the bank. It's fast. It's amazing. However, Mary Kris seems to accomplish the same tasks with pen and paper checks in considerably less time.

Because we are so busy, everyone wants to save time. In truth, we are greatly blessed. In our abundance we have too many things and too many things to do. To get a handle on the crush of things in my life I made a list of what I wanted to do--my life goals. The list was about as far as I got. As soon as the list was written, another most important task evicted my life goals. That most important task was superseded by another more urgent task. The more urgent got scheduled behind the shortest. The shortest task got put on hold by the last interruption. It happens all the time. For example, I had my whole evening planned and then Rusty, our dog, interrupted our evening by getting himself lost. He's back. He's fine now, though I'm not sure Mary Kris and I have completely recovered. I don't think I'm really to blame. Sometimes events take on a life of their own and get out of control. Here's how it happened.

It was a wonderful, peaceful summer evening. Dusk had arrived. Mary Kris was gossiping with the neighbors. I was doing guy things in the garage. Rusty was my constant companion and shadow. He was always by my side, offering advice, listening attentively, not arguing, just being a general, man's best friend. Occasionally his nose would pick up something interesting on the wind, and he might need to leave to investigate it. There was a cute poodle on the other side of the block, and if he ever left the yard it was because she had been put out on her rope, and I'd find the two of them playing chase within the limits of her tether.

I was done in the garage. All my guy things were completed and put away. OK, OK, "most" of my guy things were completed and put away. OK, OK, none were completed, but they were neatly organized in continuing projects. OK, OK, the garage was a mess. Stuff was strewn everywhere. Nothing was done, but things would keep. I was out of time.

Time to quit. I left the garage with Rusty a couple feet behind me and pressed the button to close the garage door. The door came down behind me locking Rusty in the garage. I didn't notice. I wandered about the front yard checking distracting things like the garbage (it was safe), and the dandelions (they were still healthy and doing well), and Rusty--

Hmmm. Rusty seems to have wandered off.

Mary Kris and I spent the next three hours searching the neighborhood looking for Rusty who was napping in the garage. We recruited some of our neighbors who fanned out over the neighborhood. Our enthusiasm was dampened a bit when other neighbors called the police to report that some stranger (me) was searching their back yards. Sometime after dark Mary Kris opened the garage door to find Rusty patiently wondering why he had been left in the dark.

The whole evening was shot.

The same thing happens at work. It's the last interruption, or the last person who sticks their head into my cubicle who gets the attention. Sometimes the last interruption gets interrupted by a later interruption. The whole day can be shot as the interruptions queue up. It is the definition of the "last shall be first."

So I've pretty much given up on my life goals. I'm waiting for them to downgrade to important, then urgent, get short and interrupt what I'm doing. It could happen.

I still need to get a handle on this thing we call time. It is the most important thing we have to give. When you think about it, it is really the *only* thing we have to give, because everything in the world falls into two categories:

> - Stuff: Land, property and stuff.
> - Time: Non-Stuff. Necessary for sharing, caring, and love.

We cannot give someone anything but our time. With stuff we are allowed to be the temporary caretaker of "stuff" and we accumulate stuff, pass stuff around, and exchange stuff. But stuff wears out, gets lost, or bequeathed. We can't keep stuff forever.

Time, on the other hand, is not passable and exchangeable. If I give another my time, that time is not savable, exchangeable or saleable. Widgets produced during that time may be exchanged, but the time itself is gone except for a memory. One way we are tricked into surrendering our time is to accept a pittance (sometimes called a salary) in exchange. We are exchanging temporary stuff for precious time.

As we get older, time becomes more valuable and seems to speed up. I've found two plausible theories on why time goes faster as you get older. One theory is: **Time as a Percentage of Your Life**. When you are two years old, one year is half of your life, which is equivalent to twenty-five years for someone who is fifty. So if you tell a two-year-old to wait a year for another birthday, it is the same as telling a 50-year-old to wait 25 years.

Expand this thought to smaller creatures. For example, the fruit fly lives its entire life (birth, growth, reproduction, death) in the space of two weeks. For them, time really "flys." In the space of a human eye blink, fruit fly children grow molars and learn to drive. I was explaining this to Mary Kris as the reason why insects are able to fly when it is raining. Because their short lives are running so quickly, things around them move relatively slowly. For example, insects can see raindrops falling and get out of the way--an excellent theory.

"Then why can't they see my Jeep coming?" She asked, bringing a fresh perspective to my scientific theory.

My other theory is the "**Over Committed**" theory. We get over-committed because we want to do everything. We volunteer for everything because we are able to do *anything*, but not *everything*. We keep volunteering (or being volunteered) until there is no time left. Then we are forced to fail to complete things because we are over-committed. Every time someone comes to us and pleads for something so simple and inconsequential that it seems mean-spirited to say "no," and we say "OK," we become more over-committed. Once over-committed, our time is not our own, and it races faster and faster leaving us wondering when we lost control.

When I visit the cabin, time seems to slow down because there I'm not over-committed. When I'm there, I have nothing to do but enjoy. There are no honey-do lists, or job jars. There are no phone calls or beepers, faxes or computers that own me. There are no kids carping candy and no sales people selling siding. Any of these time thieves living in the vicinity own other people, but not me. That's why vacations are so valued--you leave your commitments (and your time thieves) behind.

A friend of mine didn't own a cabin and experienced the same time slowdown right where he lived by declaring it a cabin weekend. Being at his virtual cabin-at-home he would turn off the cell phone and beeper and take the phone off the hook. He would ignore the grass, the painting, the laundry, the cleaning, and the bills. These were all things at home. Things he couldn't do and remain at his virtual cabin.

It's very easy to become over-committed. Even at the cabin where time has slowed I know how to speed it up. I stand on the dock at the lake. It's a clear, quiet spring morning. Dew covers everything. Disappearing wisps of ground fog cling to the opposite tree-sheltered shore by tentacles as they are lifted off the reflecting lake and into nothingness. I look around at the quiet beauty and wish I were a painter, and a photographer, and a biologist, a forester, hydrologist and a dozen other life-filling careers before I catch myself.

That's how we become over-committed--when we want to spend more time than we have. Once we have committed ourselves to more hours than a day gives, we drop into time-indebtedness, and we run out of time.

Everything in this world demands a chunk of time--everything from the cat to my computer. Computers are supposed to save you time, and they do amazing things--as long as you watch them. Computers, like kids and mates, want undivided attention. The instant I take my eyes off my computer it hangs, and I get the Blue-Screen-of-Death. My computer is really no different than anything else in my life. Where I put my time (my attention and energy) things prosper. If I go to the club and exercise, my body reflects that effort, but the lawn needs mowing. If I work on the house, my finances suffer. If I organize and plan my finances my writing suffers. If I find time to write, my career marks time. If I work hard at my job, my family gets neglected. If I devote myself to my family, my friends party without me. If I hang out with my buds and eat cheese doodles and burgers, my body notices. And I haven't even mentioned getting a full night's sleep, politics, religion, or my life's goals. I can do anything, but not everything. Trying to do everything generally results in a feeling of "nothing."

I speak wisely on this because I am over-committed. For me, unscheduled time is as scarce as a free-ranging turkey. It exists, but not often. Time thieves are very annoyed if you have unscheduled time. They will do their best to schedule that time on something for themselves. They usually start with the courteous question, "Are you doing anything?" Of course the time thief will ask this same question whether you are meditating in a hammock on a warm summer's day, or if you are elbow deep into a brain surgery. "Are you busy right now?" You have to schedule unscheduled time or you will never have any time to do nothing. That's the nice thing about going to a cabin hidden in the deep woods. It makes it harder for the time thieves to find you.

A serendipitous way to get time is to get a visit from the time banker. The time banker gives you time when someone cancels something. The wonderful thing about a cancellation is that you may get an unscheduled evening, or even a whole weekend to enjoy. And if the cancellation happens late enough, the time thieves are off hunting for unscheduled time elsewhere.

Unfortunately, you have to wait for the irregular visits from the time banker. The time bank isn't a place you can visit. You can't initiate a time bank withdrawal, only a time loan. The only reason you might cancel something is because you have something more urgent. That's a time loss. You then have the more urgent task, plus the rescheduled task.

The other end of wanting to do *everything* is needing to do *something*. We all need a purpose, and we all want to contribute to life. We each must do something with the time we've been allowed, even Brownie. Brownie was a little yellow ball of turkey fuzz who grew into an over-sized, forty-pound turkey dinner. Somehow Brownie was granted a pardon, and he spent a lifetime wandering the farm. Brownie had time on his hands. He slept in the doghouse with the German shepherd, and there discussed life and philosophy. The shepherd was getting old and needed an apprentice. Brownie needed something to do, so the shepherd taught Brownie farm security and how to be the official greeter. Brownie did a nice blend of the two jobs. A car would arrive. Brownie would alert the farm with the gobble alarm. Then he'd do a turkey trot up to the car and begin the feather tricks to make himself twice his already substantial size. He would submit to head pats and goiter handling before he would herd you off to the farmhouse. That was where he kept the members of his flock.

Brownie was a victim of his upbringing. Brownie had never seen another turkey. Nevertheless, turkeys are groupies and like company. Brownie adopted us humans as family despite our permanent molting and poor feathers. The challenge for Brownie was what to do with the time on his wings. After completing the security function and being the best darn greeter for a country mile, Brownie's goiter and head would start to change colors. He would drain all the blood out of his baldhead and goiter and both would turn cool and become a translucent white. Then he would flood his face with oxygen-rich blood and become a brilliant red. The blood would be trapped in the goiter and turn blue as the oxygen dissipated. Then the blood would be discharged, and the cycle would start again. This white-red-blue cycle was the first clue that free-ranging Brownie, who had imprinted on humans, was becoming amorous. Then his feathers would begin to vibrate and his tail would fan. When the drumming started, Brownie was ready to be about his turkey business.

Now this was no problem if you were an adult, but if you were a three-foot child, a forty-pound, strutting, drumming, amorous turkey could not be ignored. There were several years at the farm when no one under four feet tall could go outside alone.

It was Thanksgiving at the farm. I was in the kitchen enjoying all the snacks set out before the big dinner, so I was a bit late getting to the porch door to greet my sister Rita. Rita had just arrived with a car full of little kids. To the kids, Brownie was as big as an ostrich. If you've been to the zoo and have had a nine-foot ostrich eye your bag of popcorn, you would back away with no little concern. Now imagine yourself in the yard with the ostrich and the ostrich eyeing you. As

I opened the porch door, Rita was shouting, "Run!" to the little ones while she provided turkey interference. The little ones charged toward the house in a pack. Brownie outflanked Rita and came trotting to the porch as the last of the little ones escaped into the safety of Grandma's house. Rita then stomped past me muttering disappointment that Brownie had not been invited to our Thanksgiving dinner. I scooped up Brownie and carried him to the barn where he was locked for the rest of the holiday.

We all need a purpose in life. Brownie tried to make the best of his circumstances and did his best to protect the farm and show his affection for the rest of his flock. Like Brownie, I also have to decide how to spend my time. Like Brownie, am I spending my time in the best way possible? For example, is it better to spend my time working or playing? I am paid for my work. Is "work" better than "play" since society values "work" enough to pay me for it? Or was my time better spent on Beaver Creek, standing below the dam with the cool water rushing around my ankles; threading an angle worm onto a hook and spending a sunny afternoon catching or not catching; eating baloney sandwiches; talking or not talking; thinking or not thinking; but being?

Which is better? Which is more memorable? And is "memorable" a criteria for value? In the scheme of my life, is that sunny afternoon, fishing in youthful innocence more important than the four meetings I attended, the memo I wrote and the twenty-three e-mails I answered at work last Tuesday? I will forever remember the times my brothers and I spent fishing, but I haven't a clue what those meetings were about or who attended--although I could go look it up. Documentation is the distinction of the technocrat. I know where, when, what, and how. The "why" seems to have escaped me and seems never to be asked.

Here it is, one of our beautiful Minnesota fall days. Today I'm basking in the sun, face toward the red-yellow light filtering through my closed eyelids. My office-cold, air-conditioned body soaking in the last of the summer heat like a grateful earth facing a drought-ending shower. Is it better to work at my desk on abstract computer logic, or is it better to lie here in the sun feeling the breeze comb the hairs on my arm as I lie in this red-yellow brilliance, listening to Mozart, and thinking about free-ranging turkeys?

I think the question requires more consideration. I'm going to close my eyes for just 3½ seconds and consider it. It will be just a small withdrawal from the time bank. If it looks as if I have fallen asleep, that is just a ruse, a disguise I'll use to throw off the time thieves. After all, I'm sure they would never interrupt a nap. But first I have to see who is at the front door.

Body Language
(And other unintended Communications)

Body Language
(And Other Unintended
Communications)

I don't know if I should be allowed in public. I'm well behaved (fairly). I don't make obnoxious noises (intentionally). I don't act weird (too weird) or offend people (too often). People invite me back (sometimes). I'm an average-average, but I should not be allowed in public, not because of how I affect other people, but because of how I judge other people.

I try not to do it. I'll be minding my own business and someone walks in with a different colored shirt. Before he can sit down he has been categorized, containerized, evaluated, estimated, discombobulated, rearranged and put back together. Between his arrival and the time he sits down, he may be a totally different person. One glance and I know everything there is to know about this person. I know his politics and his religion. I have determined his character, whether he is a dog or cat person, and whether he is likely to put ketchup on his eggs.

I try not to do it. I spend half my time compartmentalizing people and the other half (the too-late half) mentally apologizing. It isn't that I think badly of others. It's more that I can't resist forming an opinion.

I try not to do it, but then someone walks into the restaurant carrying a Bible, my mind is out the gate like a greyhound after a rabbit.

Perhaps I'm confusing judging with reading body language. Back on the farm this wasn't a problem. It was a necessity. There you needed to read body language. If you didn't know what it meant when a horse laid its ears down on its neck and hopped its rear feet six inches forward like a cocked gun, you'd figure it out during your walk back from the next county. If you didn't pay attention when a cow arched her back, you could be pouring her lesson out of your boots.

Reading body language was important. We could tell by the way the hen cocked her head and looked down her beak that she was about to give you a blood test if you reached for her eggs. And we waited in the car when visiting neighbors until the farmer kicked his watchdogs off the fender of Dad's car and sent them yelping around the corner of the house. The dogs' body language was loud and obvious, and we waited for their message to change before we got out of the car--except at Uncle Julius'. There, Julius' hairless Mexican Chihuahua named Pepper would wait shivering under the car until you put out a tender ankle.

Reading body language worked on people also. After a week of predicting animal intentions, we'd pile the ten of us into our six-passenger, green '55 Buick for Sunday mass. While everyone would kneel in head-bowed, silent reverence, I watched the Communion processional, which to me was the parade of life. I knelt and watched everyone from the very young to the very old parade past. The injured farmer protecting his arm, the old man in a walker, the toddler in his mother's arms staring in big eyed stillness as the priest gave the child a blessing instead of the host. I noticed the teenagers' cool irreverence and the profound innocent reverence of the nine-year-old. As several generations of a family took their turn at the Communion railing, you could fast-forward an infant's life and see what they would look like in eighty years. Or, go in reverse and see the old man's face in his grandchildren.

I work downtown now. Downtown is like a magnet for the different people. There are many ways to be one of the *different* people. You can look differently; talk differently; believe differently; live differently; work differently; see differently--but different from what? Why different from me, of course. I can justify declaring others as "different" because it's a relative declaration. I'm as different from them as they are from me.

This downtown area affords me a chance to meet some of these different people. I was startled on this morning's bus ride to town. I was seated next to a stranger, younger and quieter than me. I rode in silence, respecting hers. I watched the traffic and enjoyed the ride. The buildings grew tall, the traffic thick. Downtown had arrived. It was time. It was quick. She signaled the driver. He pulled to the curb. She showed her intention without speaking a word. Body language is the basic common denominator between people of differences.

Downtown you see every flavor of physical differences. It is as though some of the bodies were assembled from leftover or mismatched parts. The left side doesn't match the right side or the top doesn't match the bottom. They have long legs and short arms, or long arms and short legs. Faces you can't believe because they look fake or phony--either too beautiful or too ugly, too powerful or too serene. Faces that startle you--like the drunken biker who offered to kill me "in a heartbeat." He was searching for his love. She was a topless dancer who traveled the country. He had lost her to the gaze of others and now he was lost and angry, and drunk.

Right there at the bus stop was a beggar sitting in front of our Lady of Mercy Catholic Church with his sign that said, "Please don't disturb. Help raise money for our Lady. Your prayers will be answered." I walked closer, careful not to disturb him. He noticed me. "It's OK. You can disturb me. I'm not praying now." He was a wonderfully clean and colorful beggar with a red bandana on his head, a carrot orange beard and a yellow and red flowered gypsy shirt, sitting cross-legged in dayglow green plastic shoes. In excellent conversation he said, "I raise money for our Lady by praying for your petitions in exchange for money. Your prayers will be answered, and 30% percent of all donations are given directly to Our Lady." He then launched into an eclectic philosophy about life and faith, people and places, good and evil that became a blur. It was interrupted when the good pastor came out and insisted that he do his begging elsewhere. "I usually do my praying over on the mall," the beggar said, "but today I thought I'd try here, closer to Our Lady." I could tell from the pastor's body language that the eviction was a difficult task. The pastor persisted and shooed him off before I was able to give the colorful pray-meister my dollar and request my prayer.

Downtown has bodies of every kind and shape and size and color. There are faces that look like shriveled potato heads, and faces pinched and scarred with pain and memories. If you look, you see the stress lines and crows' feet, and that occasional joy. On my bus ride home a grandmother with no teeth and a face that modeled for the art fair's pinched-nylon-stocking-faces, grabbed me with her eyes, and locked me in conversation for the duration of the bus ride. This little lady was loaded down like a packhorse. She was just a tiny wisp of a woman. Her backpack, bundles, bags, and herself squeezed into the bus seat with me, and she sat perched on one cheek, the other hanging out into the aisle. I ended perched on one cheek also. Her packages claiming the greater portion of the bench seat between us.

It was Thursday, Farmer's Market Day at the downtown mall. She showed me her purchases, which included a bag of green beans. She noticed I wasn't paying attention. Green beans will do that to me. I can't imagine anyone paying for green beans. Ever since the three summers we spent raising and hand-picking acres of green beans, I haven't been able to fully appreciate green string beans. That was a hard way to farm. My busing companion noticed my attention had drifted. Our one-cheek-apiece seats put us almost face-to-face, and she paused in the middle of relating her plans for the beans. Her black eyes waited for my attention to return before she continued with her other purchases.

My body language must be very obvious. I sometimes think people can read my mind. It's as though my private thoughts roll across my forehead like a time-and-temperature clock. "This is boring," it flashes, and my companion pauses. "Pay attention," I tell myself and my companion expounds on the strange weather we've had recently. "I want off!" my sign flashes, my face glazed.

"Where do you get off?" she asks. She is getting off ten blocks before me.

"Guilt, GUILT, **GUILT!**" My sign flashes, and I sit fully on the seat for the last ten blocks mentally kicking myself in my already sore behind for being less than congenial.

As grandmother collected her stuff and disappeared inside her load draped around her, I heroically asked, "Do you need any help?" but my sign flashed, "Please say No," and she left. She left me noticing that there have been hundreds of bus rides that I slept through, or read through, but interestingly enough, it was the one I shared with her that was memorable--miserable, but memorable. Miserable only because I didn't want to be engaged in conversation. I had looked forward all day to a nap on the bus, but instead she gave me a memorable ride as she shared herself with me.

The walls we erect to hide ourselves, to protect who we think we are can be too easily broken, and too easily scaled. Everything we might want to know about each other is displayed if we take the time to look. Our history is evident in how we protect our wounds or carry our pain. Our heritage is displayed in the color and shape of our bodies. Our opinions are exposed in how we decorate our bodies. Our thoughts are revealed by the message board on our foreheads. Our attitudes are broadcast by how we carry our bodies. And if this isn't enough to know about each other, just ask and listen. If you listen long enough, after they have told you everything they want you to know, they will tell you everything they don't want you to know.

No. I should probably avoid going out in public. Not so much because of what I think of other people, as what other people think of me. Others seem to be able to read my thoughts and me more easily than I read theirs. I just hope they don't judge me too badly when I put ketchup on my eggs.

The Furnace
(It's not as easy as it looks)

The Furnace
(It's not as easy as it looks)

I think my life is becoming more organized. Here it is March, and I still have the gloves I purchased last fall. Amazing. This is a feat that I have never accomplished. I generally go though many pairs of gloves and mittens each winter. Usually I lose just one, the right-handed one, and I end up wearing two mismatched, left-handed gloves until I can buy a new matching set, or I keep one hand in my pocket.

I think it is best I mention my success now. Spring is still weeks away and I may not have my success to brag about by then.

I suppose my tendency to lose one glove goes back to the days on the farm. Having a matched set of gloves wasn't important or always possible. If a new set of gloves appeared, it was quickly worn out as it went from hands to hands as we each took our turn outdoors. Then, since everyone was right-handed, the right-hand gloves wore out first. To find two left-handed gloves without holes was better than ones with vents.

Between wearings, our gloves would dry on the hot water radiators in the house. The first one dressed got the gloves without holes. Of course, first choice off the radiator was dry gloves or mittens--with or without holes--left or right.

Aside from drying mittens and hats, the radiators defrosted people. In winter I'd struggle in from the cold, grasp the toasty radiator with my blue fingers, shove my frozen feet under the bottom and stand spread-eagled against the grill. Once in an effort to get closer, I climbed on top of the radiator and tried to nap. Napping on the bare metal ridges of a radiator was even less comfortable than sleeping on a bony cow's ribcage.

Throughout my childhood and adolescence, the radiators were kept warm by several methods. When I was smallest, about three or four, we used high-sulfur content coal that came in chunks. The coal burned away leaving clinkers in the furnace that looked like misshapen pig iron. When they cooled, the clinkers were crushed and sprinkled on the lane as homemade gravel.

Tending a furnace that was growing clinkers was a frequent and regular chore. Dad pulled the clinkers from the furnace with a long-handled, three-fingered, mechanical hand with an opposable thumb. The clinkers glowed red but quickly turned dark when he put them in a metal bushel basket. Dad turned off the basement light, and we watched in the darkness. The basket of clinkers gave up waves of soft red energy. Dad showed me how to spit on the clinkers causing a black spot to appear on the hot clinkers and make them complain and spit back. Dad started shouting and turned on the light when I peed on the basket of clinkers. Pungent, choking, urine-sulfur steam hit our noses. "Put that thing away!" Dad ordered. He grabbed the basket's rope handles and moved the stinking steaming basket outside the house.

The next year I was a little bigger, and we upgraded our furnace fuel to a higher-grade coal that came in granules that could be poured.

A red dump truck heaped with blackness backed up to the house and poured itself into the basement.

Coal is really quite beautiful. Under the glow of the coal room light, the coal glinted like a room full of black diamonds. I thought this granular coal inferior since it didn't produce clinkers in interesting shapes, but it did work great as black chalk and I drew pictures on the floor, doors, walls, stairs or any flat surface. It had a rich oil-soaked texture that came off on my skin so I used it to paint my hands and face. I had never seen a black person, but when I went upstairs, Mom was sure I wasn't one of her children and tried to send me away. The coal made such a good disguise, it took some scrubbing to convince Mom that I was really her son and not some runaway. Mom seemed really surprised to find me under all that blackness. Mom hugged me and told me how glad she was to have her little boy back again. It was so much fun fooling mom that I went right back downstairs to the coal room and put on my black boy disguise again.

It wasn't as much fun the second time.

In addition to coal we also burned firewood. Actually, I think burning firewood was another excuse for Dad to hitch up the team of horses to the sled, load it with his freshly sharpened double bite ax, a sledge, a couple wedges, the chain saw, and head for the woods.

The fun part for me was watching the trees come crashing down. Each year Dad cut down a couple trees that became next year's firewood. He took the smaller branches off the trunk and cut up the branches into firewood. The horses would stand patiently and wait until it was their turn to be hitched to the main trunk of the fallen tree and skid the log to the lumber pile.

Dad always saved the trunk of the tree for lumber which was cut into rough planks that sat in the sun and cured naturally for a couple years. Our small woods was all strong oak and ironwood hickory. Both were woods that were impossible for me to build with. I treasured any small piece of store-bought pine that was soft enough for me to cut, pound, and turn into sawdust. But the hardwoods were what grew locally, and they furnished the infrastructure for any construction or maintenance done on the farm. The shop, the chicken coup, the corncrib and even the porch swing were made from home-grown lumber. Those woods that I disrespected because of their strength, we now call exotic woods; and what we now pay for one board foot, we could then have bought the whole tree.

During the logging, to keep me from turning into a little pillar of ice, Dad would build a fire that I kept fed with twigs and branches too small for furnace firewood. I stood around the fire, thawing my front while my backside froze. I dropped a length of firewood on my frozen foot. It felt like I had stuck my foot into an electric socket. The good news was that I still had some feeling in my foot. I hadn't had any news from my other foot for a while. I kick-rolled a bigger chunk of firewood over to my fire to use for a chair. The kicking was a big mistake. Each kick gave me an electrical jolt. I set up my stump-chair and stuck both feet toward the fire until the boots melted, and I gave myself a hot foot (feet).

As more of my siblings were born, our family grew, and more and more resources went for food and clothing. To reduce expenses we started using less coal and more firewood, but over the years we had pretty well thinned out the small woods north of the home buildings.

As we ran out of woods, we tried several fuels including corncobs. Then we discovered hardwood scraps from the stave mill. We'd travel to the local mill where they made wooden whiskey barrels. The scrap wood was free and clean. Each scrap piece was small enough so that we, as kids, could handle it. Duane would drive the tractor or truck pulling a wagon that we would fill with scrap wood.

The only problem with stave mill scrap wood was that it had to be cut to shorter lengths to fit in the furnace. After we stacked one end of the basement with the 4' scraps, one of us would occasionally climb on top the stack with a chain saw and cut the scraps in half to about the depth of the saw blade, or until the basement filled so full of blue exhaust from the chain saw that you couldn't breath. Between cuttings the chain saw hung around the basement waiting for another chance to attack the woodpile.

One winter Saturday when we were supposed to be outside working, but were instead watching TV, baby sister Jane who was about 5 or 6 was down tending the furnace. We had let the fire get low. Jane filled up the mouth of the furnace with the scrap wood, but there was no flame. Jane was about to discover that some small hot coals were hidden under the ashes in the bottom of the furnace. Gasoline for the chainsaw was sitting there, so Jane took a cup of the gas and threw it on the wood.

The first I knew about it, Jane appeared at the top of the basement steps with no eyelashes, singed hair, unable to speak coherently, but yammering something very urgent and pointing downstairs. I charged into the basement to find the flames going up the side of the furnace and licking at the ceiling. I closed the furnace door with my foot. That put most of the flames back in the furnace. Then I used an empty gunnysack to beat out the rest of the flames.

Not much damage was done. Our big problem was how to explain to Dad why we were watching TV when we were supposed to be outside helping Duane. The fire did result in a State fair winning 4-H safety demonstration where the topic was "The Safe Storage and Use of Fuels on the Farm." The audience especially liked it when I set some gas-soaked rags on fire. At least, I think they liked it. There was always a collective gasp when the gasoline ignited, and they were visibly pleased when I put out the flames.

I'm not sure my safety demonstration was entirely safe.

Later, after a few of us kids grew up and left home, the family became prosperous enough to bring in an LP gas tank and a new furnace. I came home from military service to find that the old monster furnace and coal bin had been replaced with a highly efficient little box smaller than a refrigerator. It wasn't a very social piece of equipment. It didn't want to be visited every couple hours and had neither a yawning mouth demanding to be fed, nor did it have a row of air vents that looked like fiery angry eyes. The coal room was swept clean and had become a storage room, although some of my drawings still survived on the walls and doors like primitive cave art. The window we used to feed the stave mill wood down into the basement has been built over by a new attached garage.

So things change, and if you hang around long enough you start seeing the same things again. For example, a few years ago everyone thought that heating with firewood was great fun, economic, ecological, and great exercise. It seemed easy. I tried it. My first house had a fireplace so I bought a load of unsplit knotty oak firewood. I had watched Dad easily split large blocks of wood with a single clean swing. After hours of arguing with my small pile of firewood I never mastered log splitting. I did, however, figure out how Dad stayed warm while I was freezing next to the fire. I got more heat and warmth out of that firewood trying to split it, than I ever did burning it in the fireplace.

As a kid you never quite appreciate what your parents have done for you until you try to do it yourself. Providing simple comfort and warmth is quite an accomplishment.

Tools, Toasters & Trolls[3]
(Or: Advice You Always Ignore)

My car's blinkers have gone on the blink. Like every machine, they gave me fair warning. I've noticed that none of our faithful mechanical servants ever quit without warning. Back on the farm, the hay bailer and corn picker always issued a high pitched squeal that you either greased or later replaced. The tires on the hay wagons always puffed out their cheeks protesting the extra layers of bails before they burst. No tractor ever stranded you in the field without a lot of coughing and wheezing that you ignored. There is always some ticking, grinding, whistling or clanking communiqué from the machine first. We may ignore our machines' pleadings or not understand the complaints, but usually, as in my case, I knew and ignored the message. So my blinkers quit.

Before they walked off the job they changed their song from a rhythmic on-off, on-off, on-off, to an oon-off, oon-ooff, o-oon-o-o-ff. Then after a couple weeks, they issued one final o-o-o-off.

---

[3] Story published in AutoWeek, Crain Communications Inc., March 1-7, 1999, "The Quick Fix goes the Way of the Free Lunch"

No problem. I'm a guy. I can fix things.

I knew the blinker bulbs were OK and I also knew by the last pleadings from my blinkers that it wasn't the fuse. I went to my local Big Guy Auto store and bought a "flasher."

A flasher is what turns your blinkers on and off and is also what makes the on-off sound. It looks like a three-prong electrical plug except it is silver. It is about the size of a nickel. It looks like six nickels stacked on a three-legged milking stool with very short legs and a very thick seat. Installation is as simple as plugging a toaster into an electrical socket.

There was only one problem I soon found out: the manufacturer of my fine GM product took extra pains to hide the inner workings of the car from wanna-be-mechanics.

I don't know how I knew it, but I knew that the flasher was under the dash. Perhaps it was my "guy" genes that let me know where the flasher lived.

Auto designers put things under the dash because they are either mean or stupid. You have to be a contortionist to work under there. Being small or slight is only a slight advantage. No one is small enough or slight enough. I don't think the designers are stupid. They know *they* won't have to work on the car.

I assumed my preferred under-the-dash working position, which is exactly the same as when I'm driving, except my head and feet are reversed. The only thing in the same location is my butt. I get into position with my head resting on the brake pedal and now I am sure that the auto designers are not stupid, just mean.

Hmmm. No flasher. It must be on the passenger side. I get up and brush the footprints off the ceiling.

Now if I had paid attention to the warning complaints of my blinkers, I could just turn on the blinkers and follow the on-off, on-off sounds to the flasher. I thought the flasher could be on the passenger side since my passengers seemed to be able to hear the blinkers better than me. That would explain why my kids always notice when I drive down the freeway with my left blinker on. "Your blinker's on, Dad."

Nothing on the passenger side.

I drove back to Big Guy Auto, steeled myself and asked the big question: "Where is it? Where did GM hide the flasher?"

The parts man blinked in quiet astonishment as though I had asked him to point out the wheels on my car.

"Under the dash. Usually on the driver's side."

Ahha! They do put it on the passenger side.

Right there in the Big Guy parking lot I started looking. I had my head under the passenger side dash when a Big Guy customer came out of the store. He couldn't get into his driver's side door since I was lying in my passenger's side door.

"Whatcha look'n for?"

"Oops. Sorry. I'm trying to find the flasher for my turn signals."

"The flasher? It's under the driver's side." With that he went to show me.

He used what I considered the more difficult position for working under a dash. He knelt on the ground outside the car and turned the top part of his body 180 degrees so that his head appeared to be on backwards. In that position he looked as if he knew what he was doing. I went back to the passenger side so I wouldn't have to watch the crack of his butt being stretched out of his jeans, and so I could see what he was doing under the dash.

He was grunting and tugging on things. He covered all the same territory I had and was becoming frustrated, but he had committed himself. Guys don't ask for directions because they know they can figure it out. (They just need time). Conversely, this guy claimed to know where the flasher was, and he wasn't coming out until he found it.

He was tugging on the edges of my dash and on my wires so hard I was afraid he was going to break something. He pulled so hard on something under the dash that he did a chin-up, driving his head into the underside of the dash. Blood was trickling down his bald scalp, and I could see he was moving beyond frustration.

"Don't worry about it," I said as he tried to pry the bottom of my dash back like the lid of a partially opened can of peas. He let it spring back.

I wanted this helpful, but tenacious good Samaritan out of my dash before he disassembled my dashboard without tools. He obviously was as ignorant as me. It was our level of knowledge that coined the phrase "ignorance is bliss." In every guy's realm of experience there is an area of expertise where he knows everything. He just hasn't done much there. It might be cooking, childbearing, construction, computers, and, of course, cars. He knows everything. Just don't ask him to demonstrate that knowledge or you end up with what I have--a red-faced, bleeding, angry troll crouched under my dash.

It took some coaxing to get him to relax his grip on a fistful of wires and back away from the car.

I got his head and hips facing the same direction and the circulation returned to his legs. The bleeding stopped. I escorted the good Samaritan to his car and thanked him for his efforts.

Guys don't ask guys for directions because guys can't say, "I don't know." They seem to need to prove that they don't know.

I drove around without blinkers for a couple more weeks paralyzed by knowing that I didn't know and knowing that no one else knew either.

It was a pretty ugly time. Without blinkers I came to hate intersections. It seemed there was always someone waiting for me to go *through* the intersection, but I'd slow down and turn. I avoided looking at them.

The drivers following me were less patient when I stopped in the middle of an intersection to turn. As I waited for the traffic to clear, I could see them behind me checking for alternative lanes and pounding their steering wheels, then changing lanes and roaring past me. I was creating dangerous situations on busy city streets.

I needed blinkers. Using hand signals in a dark Minnesota winter gets you frostbite and complaints from your passengers. Plus, a hand stuck out into the dark is fairly well ignored.

I did not want to pay to have my flasher replaced. That would be like asking a handyman to plug in your toaster. Far too simple a task.

I was in having my oil changed, and I casually asked the mechanic if he knew where the flasher was hidden. He said it was under the driver's side dash hidden under a panel secured by four screws. "Do you want me to replace it?"

"No. No. Too small a task. I don't want to bother you. I'll do it."

The next Saturday I had my head on the brake pedal and my feet on the ceiling. I took out the four screws, popped out the flasher, and put in the new one.

No change. The blinkers still didn't work. I had replaced the emergency flasher, not the turn signal flasher. With the blood draining into my head I looked around under the panel I had removed. There was no second flasher, but ahha! There was a similar (but different) plug-in-thingy.

I pulled it out and drove to Big Guy Auto and headed for the Parts Department passing one of the clerks.

"Horn relay," he said as we passed in the aisle.

"What?"

"Horn relay. It looks like you have your horn relay."

"Yeah." I said. I made a big loop of the store aisles and left without talking to anyone. I replaced the horn relay and drove for a couple more weeks, enduring insults, escaping road rage, and feinting complete innocence at every intersection.

Then GM sent me a safety recall. It seems my horn cover had a tendency to fall off. True. I had two teenagers who found great joy in honking at everything. During one of my daughter's enthusiastic honkings the horn cover popped off. I disconnected the horn before replacing the cover and had been driving in peaceful silence ever since. Now the kids have grown through that phase, and it would be nice to have a horn again.

This factory recall might be a way to get my blinkers and horn repaired at the same time…and save face. With the horn recall in hand I drove to Friendly's Super Deals Auto Mart, our local auto dealer.

Auto dealers do warranty work. The blinkers were not under warranty, but I knew auto dealers were used to dealing with all the detail, trivia and minutia of satisfying new car owners. Plus it was a big operation so the mechanic would never see me, and I would not see the mechanic laughing when he got the blinker repair order.

I drove my Cavalier into Friendly's as if my time was more important than money and gave the service guy my repair list:

<u>Repair List</u>
- Factory recall: Repair horn cover
- Grease squeak in door
- Fix blinkers
- Plug in toaster

What's this?"

"Just kidding about the toaster," I said grabbing a free donut and coffee and headed for the waiting room.

The waiting room at Friendly's is a staging area for lost souls. Aside from the interminable wait and the bad TV with no remote and no on-off button, you find yourself an unwilling participant in the dealer's mind games.

The Spartan ergonomics of the waiting room are just the beginning. I have relinquished control of my car to a faceless talent. Experience has taught me that I have a less than even chance of a minor repair being completed well, and even less of a chance that I will be charged a fair price.

Friendly prefers that I abandon my car for at least a day. After all, anything that takes an entire day to complete has to be worth his outrageous prices. Friendly knows that after a day of separation from their cars, car owners are as excited as puppies when their master returns from the next room after being gone for a minute. If Friendly can get me to leave the car, I'll be so grateful when I get it back I won't complain a lot. Also, the mechanic who did the work, and most of the staff, will be gone when I pick up my car.

This time I tough it out. I wait. Finally my name is blared over the loud speaker and it is my turn with the cashier who is blissfully ignorant of auto mechanics. She presents me with a hand-scribbled bill on which the only legible items are my name and the "total due."

When I average the total due across: fixing the horn, greasing the squeaky door AND the blinkers, it's fairly reasonable for all three. A small home-equity loan should cover it.

At last I have my car back. The door doesn't make noise, the horn does, and the blinkers sing their two-note on-off song. The car seems to run better. Even the headlights burn brighter.

Driving is a joy again. I go around honking and blinking at people just for the joy of it. I once again feel fully licensed.

Hmmm. My headlight just blew. And without warning.

No problem. I can fix it. How hard can it be?

How Cold is "Cold?"
(Listen To Your Kids)

How Cold is "Cold?"
(Listen To Your Kids)

Growing up on a Minnesota farm, the experience of "Cold" was my predominate experience. Being cold generally lasted from the freezing dawns of August through late May snowstorms. If I had to summarize my major experience of puberty and adolescence in one word that was not an emotion, it would have to be "Cold."

Being a novice, but enthusiastic parent, I wanted to share my experience of "Cold" with my son, Matt. I soon found out that since we lived in the city, experiencing cold would be no easy feat. The city has thermostatically controlled furnaces, insulated buildings, skyways, and attached garages that keep you from cold. Besides, you can't just step outside to experience real cold. Sure it might bite a bit, or give you goose bumps, but to experience "Cold" you need an activity from which you can't escape, that takes hours, and totally saturates your being.

Most of the opportunities to get really cold have vanished for my son. So we (I) decided on winter camping. I had never done it. Camping is fun. Could winter camping be that different?

Actually, I can't take the full credit for the winter camping idea. Matt and I were members of a YMCA Voyageurs troop. For anyone a little weak in history, and to confirm I spelled it right, the "Voyageurs" were a group of hearty French explorers who were lost in Minnesota and Canada in the 1700s. So impressed were we with their accomplishments that we emulated their manliness and did Voyageur things like: canoeing, hiking, rock climbing, and getting lost. We must have run out of the fun things to emulate, so it was decided we would go winter camping.

The fact that we had no winter camping gear didn't seem to bother our survival instructor and leader. He said, "The reason people get cold is because they use furnaces and heavy clothing. If you want to be comfortable, you have to become acclimated to the cold. There would be no huddling around the campfire." In fact, there would be no campfire.

"If you get cold, you will do exercises to stoke the internal furnace in your body," he said. "Besides, a campfire might melt our snowhuts."

"Whoa! Whadayamean 'melt our snowhuts?' " I asked.

"We will sleep in the snow by building a snowhut. A snowhut is like an igloo only it's made differently."

"How differently?"

"Once we arrive at the campsite, our first order of business will be to make a mound of snow the size of a four-man tent (actually two dads and two sons). Snowdrifts won't work. The snow has to be compacted. Then we'll have breakfast..."

"This is before breakfast?"

"...then we'll have breakfast while the geo-thermal heat from the earth penetrates our pile of snow making it compact into one large sticky snowball."

This sounded like a great opportunity for Matt to experience "Cold," though I didn't like our leader's repeated reference to "survival training" during the pep talk.

We arrived at the campsite right after dawn. I didn't bother to mention that we had stopped for a fast-food breakfast during the drive out. We showed up wearing every piece of winter clothing we owned, plus a couple outfits from summer, and set about our first task of scraping the ground bare to release the geo-thermal energy. Then we put back the snow, making an igloo sized, heaping pile of snow.

Sure enough, after a couple hours our snow pile was ready to be hollowed out. Here was a great opportunity for "cold"--lying on your belly as you tunneled forward, lying on your back as you tunneled up, the snow ceiling falling in chunks onto your face as you chipped away raising the ceiling. I shouted and a couple dads dragged me out of the hut by my ankles. I stood up to brush the snow off my face and succeeded in wedging it down my neck. Another dad disappeared (except for his boots) into the hut and continued digging.

I looked around for Matt. He was off with the other kids playing a game of boot hockey. That would never do. How will he ever get a good sense of cold if he is getting all heated up having fun? He should be standing here with snow down his neck, digging or watching.

By lunchtime we had our huts hollowed out. Ours was complete with a snow slab door so we could be sealed in. For the next couple hours each hollowed hut had a candle burning in it. The candle would produce enough heat to melt a thin layer of snow on the inside. When the candle was removed, the hut froze solid enough for a 300-pound man to stand on its dome (This was tested).

Construction done, we had the afternoon to ourselves. We hiked out onto the lake to annoy the ice fisherman. The way I figured it, the ice fisherman were so bored they would appreciate a troop of ten-year-olds to whom they could show off their catch. Who would have guessed they'd be so grouchy? You'd think it was our fault the fish stopped biting.

Standing around on the ice was good. On the way back each step was giving me that old familiar electric shock you get just before your feet freeze solid. Excited, I asked Matt if he was getting cold.

"No."

I did the electric stomp over to our leader. He said I could warm up my feet by doing calisthenics or playing boot hockey. If that didn't warm them, we'd have to put them into someone's armpits. The group of dads I was with seemed to shrink away from me. We headed to the boot-hockey rink. One of the dads confided that he was so cold he didn't think his armpits could warm up anyone's feet.

Our leader gave us strict orders not to work up a sweat. Anyone caught sweating would have to change into dry, long underwear. The thought of having to change underwear with Old Man Winter waiting for exposed extremities to freeze off kept the boot-hockey game at a mellow level.

After boot hockey we went to check out the snow huts. Two had collapsed. We felt bad for the dads and sons. They would have to sleep inside tonight. There was some friendly bantering that they had collapsed their huts intentionally so they could sleep inside, but I knew they were just kidding.

Our snowhut was a snow architect's dream. It was prefect except where it had sagged a little on one side. The dome inside was perfect: smooth as ice, and hard as ice as it curved from the top of the dome all the way down to the condensation-catch-trough built out of snow-turned-ice around the perimeter bottom.

Inspection finished, there was nothing to do except wait for dark, calisthenics, and seal the two dads and two sons into each hut.

Personally, I was a little apprehensive about our hut mates. They were nice enough. The son was a smaller version of the dad who was a large man. The doorway into our hut took his largeness into consideration.

The consensus of our small community of dads was that my team was quite fortunate. The extra mass provided by our hut mates would generate extra body heat, and body heat was the only heat we had.

My only concern aside from space was that this dad was a prodigious snorer. We had discovered this on previous camping trips where our entire troop and the surrounding woods were kept awake as sounds of large equipment with bad engines rolled though our camp. My concern wasn't that we would be entombed inside an ice dome that reflected and amplified the tiniest sound, or the fact that our sons and we would be tiled shoulder-to-shoulder across the hut floor. No, my real concern was that his snoring would cause stress fractures in the dome and cause it to collapse on us sometime during the dark, cold night.

After calisthenics, our leader began the entombing of the father-son pairs. Too soon, it was our turn.

Since body heat was our only source of heat, the hut was intentionally small. There was no room to stand, though you might accomplish a cramped hunker.

Our leader said, "Survival required the efficient utilization of body heat." It would be inefficient to have a larger hut with more room. We were really lucky and would be very comfortable since we had no energy-wasting, empty air spaces.

No more delays. Time for bed.

The other son went in first and wedged up against the outside wall. The large dad blanketed the center of the hut, and I claimed a spot next to him. All that was left was to get Matt in and seal up the door. Our leader hunted up Matt. It didn't take too long. It didn't matter much how long it took. I wasn't going anywhere until dawn. I laid there on my back staring at the ice dome, feeling the cold start to seep up into my body. The mats and insulation our survival instructor said would be sufficient seemed a bit thin right now. I wondered if I should have done another dozen jumping-jacks to stoke my internal furnace. Matt had been off with the other kids romping in the moonlight and snow. He stuck his head in the hut and peered over our three sets of feet. His face was flushed and his eyes were bright from playing at ten-year-old speed.

"Hi." I said. "I've got your sleeping bag right here. Come on. Hop in."

"There's no room." He said.

"Sure there is. Crawl in. Crawl right over the top of us."

"Where's my sleeping bag?"

"Here. Right next to me. You probably can't see it from there. It's under this ledge. The hut ceiling sagged a little bit so the ceiling is a little low, but you have a neat little space just the perfect size for you."

"No way. I'm not sleeping under there." And he disappeared from the hut door.

Our leader's face replaced Matt's over our feet. "What happened?" he asked.

"Matt doesn't think there is enough room for him to sleep under this ledge. Will you go get him?"

We waited a couple minutes. I rolled slightly to one side. It was beginning to feel like I was lying on an ice pack. I was. My backside was getting slightly numb, and it had only been minutes. Maybe I should do a few pushups while we wait.

After a couple minutes Matt reappeared over our feet. "What? I'm not going to sleep under there," he said without waiting for an answer.

No amount of coaxing or threatening or promising could get Matt into the hut. The longer I laid there, the colder I got, and the less convincing my logic became. Finally, with an insincere expression of regret, I unzipped my sleeping bag and followed Matt to the cabin where the dads and sons whose huts had collapsed were assigned to sleep.

I slept well that night. The gas-fired furnace that shared the bunkhouse with us came on frequently that sub-zero night. I woke a couple times and watched the shadows dance between the soft warm light the flames cast on the floor. I figured that by now, if we had stayed in the hut, my backside would be beyond numb.

I slept very well.

In the morning we went to the lodge for breakfast. Most of the hut sleepers were already there. They were all very quiet. Most were like frozen zombies, not quite sure if they had survived. After some coffee and hot chocolate, they were able to relate how the night went. One hut broke camp in the middle of the night and returned to the city. Another hut had spent most of the night sleeping in their car with the engine running. The less coherent ones sat there, slowly defrosting, preferring not to remember. Of course, there was one dad who came bursting in, declaring it a totally invigorating and wonderful experience. No one challenged him. I wondered where he really spent the night.

As everyone thawed back to life, I marveled at the hut sleepers' accomplishment, and I complained about not getting to sleep in a snow hut. After all, I was taught not to brag.

So, Matt never really got to experience "Cold." It was a dandy of an opportunity. But, this was not the first time or the last time that my son Matt and I have disagreed about what is best. There will probably be others, but I've learned that he does very often make very good decisions.

I slept very well.

Sunrise Surprise
(Real Beauty)

It happened on a Minnesota morning just after sunrise.

The farmland lacked its traditional blanket of snow that could transform all into a winter wonderland. It was quiet. It was cold. I was driving alone. It reminded me of a night years ago when I was delivering steel to Minneapolis from Chicago and found myself driving the Minneapolis freeways at 4AM. I was alone. No one was on the freeway. No cops. No trucks. No milkmen. I was alone, which struck me as "quiet." The city was completely quiet. Not empty, but quiet.

This bare November rural land had that same quiet: a stillness; a hesitation; like a car between gears. The world was for an instant, still, like a body between breaths. Then it happened. On this cold November morning, still grateful from Thanksgiving, traveling on a full tank of gas with hot coffee and good tunes, I'd been watching the sun rise from behind a far horizon. I drove southeast and the sun rose at a convenient angle and I watched it ascend into a perfect, ruddy ball with a cloud strip placed artistically across its equator giving it depth and enhancing the fire. The sun rose above the horizon's cloud crack framed by the distant Minnesota bluffs, and I noticed again the quiet almost like the stillness before the start of a play. Not emptiness. Not without energy, just attentive quiet.

Ahead, ghost-black silhouettes punctuated the horizon. Not the flat black of paper silhouettes, but black with indefinable depth; blackness hinting at unseen texture suggesting hidden features in the silhouettes.

That's when it happened as I drove across this frosty Minnesota country. The road swung south, then east, and I topped one of the rolling knolls. There, looking out across miles of open land, with backlit ground fog and silhouetted barns and silos, was an artist's reality.

The sun itself was hidden above the clouds, but a minor cloud fissure seeped light into the surreal landscape. It was one of those movie moments where the music swells, the angels sing, and God speaks.

As I drove, I watched the perfect balance of light, land and fog shift as I viewed it from different angles. I watched it shift and change as the sun rose, and the fog burned off.

As I drove into that painting of land and sky and spirit, it lost its unreal beauty bit by bit. When I arrived where the beauty was, the land had returned to November green, November brown and November sleep. I wondered where the beauty went. I drove out the backside of that painting and wondered how many times our perspective; our closeness to a situation prevents us from seeing the magic in where we are? How often do we live in the details and fail to see our beauty, our contribution to the big picture?

So here I am, the sun is an hour up. The frost is gone. The cloudbank on the horizon has cleared. The grass has changed from crystals, to polished dew, to dry brown.

And I wonder if this normal, average, no adjective, sleeping land still looks as magical from that first knoll-top vantage point miles behind me? I should drive back and check. It's important. Are we always beautiful? Or are we only beautiful when viewed from one perspective? Is our real beauty as a people, as a nation, as a land, expressed only in the luck of the perfect combination of light, land and temperature? Or, is our true beauty revealed when we see our relationship to the whole?

I should really drive back to that knoll top and check. It's important.

Nah--some other time. I'm on a schedule--maybe on my way back.

The End

List of Illustrations[4]

Rural Wisdom – Cover Page

I was fourteen. It was spring. The ground was soft and I was plowing the southwest forty. The tractor bogged down in a soft spot. With typical teenage reaction, I was angry that the equipment wasn't capable of the job. I kept the wheels spinning amused by the flying mud and challenged to see how fast I could "not go." Then, having hopelessly buried the wheels, fear set in when, I realized the folly of my actions. Dad arrived in the family's 1956 nine-passenger Nash Rambler. Before he did anything he documented my folly with his Polaroid camera.

---

[4] All photographs were taken by the author on a 35MM film camera except where indicated.

Fair Time
(Change), Page-xvi
1965 – Brother Mark with one of our Champion Ayrshire cows. Hard as I didn't try, I never did make it to the Champion's circle. All my brothers and sisters had more success there then I did. (Photo by Tri-State Breeders)

Prairie Trip
(Choose a Dream), Page-8
A 1985 Saturday afternoon of hand-picking sweet corn for canning. There's a job for everyone.

A Lot of Bull
(We All Want the Same Things), Page-24
1975 -- Patrick the bull. His predecessor, Clyde, is the villain in the story. Patrick, Clyde's successor, was a champion and vigorous sire despite the annoyance of the safety chain in his nose.

Cow Snoozing
(Things are the Way They're Supposed to Be), Page-34
1975 -- The barn was originally built with twenty-four stanchions plus the pens on the left to hold calves. The milking ritual always started at the far end and we milked toward the camera and the milk house.

The Swarm
(When You Lose Someone), Page-44
1978 – My dad Linus tending his hives. He maintained the hives primarily to combat his hay fever. One tablespoon of locally grown honey would completely stop all hay fever symptoms.

186

Silent Secrets
(The Value of Nothing), Page-52

1980 -- My favorite view of the family farm. It's the first view from the road whenever I return.

The Clothesline
(Remember Who You Are), Page-62

1985 – The clotheslines waiting for the dryer to fail.

The Orange Prince
(A Second Chance), Page-70

1978 – One of the farm cats. Since they are outside all winter, they grow an extra thick, extra scruffy looking fur coat.

The Nose Knot
(Differences), Page-80

1985 – Tibbs, my mom's dapple grey Arabian.

The Crush
(Perspective), Page-86

1920 –Margaret Hoffman Ernster, my grandmother. This picture is very special to me. I never knew my grandmother as a beautiful young woman. And as long as I have this picture, I can't look at a fully mature (old) person without knowing that there is a lifetime of experience and stories that I've missed. (Photo by Palen Studio, Caledonia, MN)

Where Am I?
(I Don't Understand), Page-92
1985 – Brother John, ice fishing at dawn on the Mississippi by Brownsville Minnesota. He's out checking his tip-ups after spending the night in the icehouse on the right.

When Spring Arrives
(Beliefs), Page-98
1978 – Brother Dave on the freshly painted and stenciled 1940 Farmall M.

The Jaws of My Jeans
(The Miracle), Page-126
1953 - 1955 – The author's first cousin Sister Mary Margo when she was a novice studying to become a Franciscan nun. The picture was probably taken at the motherhouse, Assisi Heights, in Rochester Minnesota. Sister Marga has recently celebrated her Golden Jubilee, fifty years of service to the Franciscans. Photographer is unknown.

Time Thieves
(What to do with Time???), Page-136
1983 – Me, hoping for a short nap during a trail ride through southern Minnesota. My son Matt and his cousins Ryan and Joey have designs on my nap time. (Photo taken on author's camera. Photographer unknown)

Body Language
(And other unintended Communications), Page-148
1977 – My daughter Miki lolling on the grass with all the carefree innocence of a three year old.

The Furnace
(It's not as easy as it looks), Page-156

1960 – South of the farm, just across the Iowa border, was a Whiskey Barrel Stave mill. My dad took this picture during one of our forays to the mill to collect scrap wood for the furnace. Photo by Linus Ernster.

Tools, Toasters & Trolls
(Or: Advice You Always Ignore), Page-166

A pen and ink drawing by my son Matt.

How Cold is "Cold?"
(Listen To Your Kids), Page-172

1988 – The morning after the winter camping trip. My son Matt and his fellow Voyageurs are playing "King of the Hut." The huts, after curing in the sub-zero night, were able to support the weight of a three hundred pound man.

Printed in the United States
73190LV00004B/19-36